Decorative
Knot

Kim Sang Lan

Acknowledgements

I would like to express my gratitude to Kim Hee-Jin for giving me such a solid and thorough grounding in Korean decorative knot craft.

I would also like to thank Cho Seong Chang, former director of the Korean Cultural Centre, and all those who have supported me throughout my journey, in particular all the members of the ADAC (Association for the Development of Cultural Activities), the Korean Cultural Centre and the Musée Guimet in Paris.

Last but by no means least, I would like to thank my students, with whom I have tied lasting bonds of friendship and whose confidence and patience have given me the strength to forge ahead.

Decorative tassel with traditional motifs, by the author.

A DAVID & CHARLES BOOK

Copyright © 2006 Groupe Fleurus 15–17 rue Moussorgski 75895 Paris Cedex 18 France Originally published in France as *L'art du Maedup Noeuds Coréens*

David & Charles is an F+W Publications Inc. company 4700 East Galbraith Road Cincinnati, OH 45236

First published in the UK in 2008

A catalogue record for this book is available from the British Library.

ISBN-13: 978-0-7153-2922-1 paperback
ISBN-10: 0-7153-2922-7 paperback

Printed in China by SNP Leefung
for David & Charles
Brunel House   Newton Abbot   Devon

Visit our website at www.davidandcharles.co.uk

David & Charles books are available from all good bookshops; alternatively you can contact our Orderline on 0870 9908222 or write to us at FREEPOST EX2 110, D&C Direct, Newton Abbot, TQ12 4ZZ (no stamp required UK only); US customers call 800-289-0963 and Canadian customers call 800-840-5220.

Decorative
Knot Craft

Kim Sang Lan

Over 20 innovative knotting
& macramé accessories

D&C
David and Charles

Contents

An introduction to knotwork

Knots have been with us since the dawn of time and they now play a functional role in our everyday life. In the Far East, knotwork is regarded as an ancient craft passed down from generation to generation. There, knots have a predominately decorative function and are used in particular to add detail to traditional dress.

The tradition of decorative knot art began in China and spread gradually throughout Asia. At first, it seems that knotting had a practical rather than aesthetic role. But over time, knotting techniques became more and more sophisticated, new motifs were created and each country developed its own tradition. And this was how Korean knot craft, known as *maedup* ('knot' in Korean), grew into an artistic discipline of its own. The Chinese names for the various knots are often associated with abstract notions, whereas in Korean the knots take their names from nature and everyday life. Since its beginnings, Korean knotwork has reflected its people's conscientious way of life and

Traditional tassel by the author, with jade bead.
Featured knots: ginger, ring and double connection.

particular attention to detail. Today it is thought to comprise around 40 basic motifs.

The earliest evidence of Korean knotwork is said to date back to the time of the Three Kingdoms of Korea, from the 1st century BC to the 7th century AD. We have pictorial evidence of knotted cord used to decorate belts, ceremonial hats and flags. At first a symbol of royal authority and luxury, knotwork gradually filtered through to all layers of Korean society, enabling people to decorate their clothing, everyday objects (purses, fans and musical instruments) and their homes.

Knotwork also became part of everyday life for Koreans because it was used for religious purposes, to make Buddhist ornaments. Even today, knots remain an essential part of traditional dress and Koreans often give them away as good luck charms. Now an art form of its own and a valued part of Korea's cultural heritage, knot craft is under continual research at specialist institutes there.

Traditional tassel by the author, with
embroidered lotus flower medallion.
Featured knots: ginger, ring and double connection.

Basic equipment

Cord

Knots were traditionally made using silk cord, often spun and hand-dyed by the artist. Today, many types of cord suitable for making up decorative knot craft designs can be found in haberdasheries and craft shops. The designs in this book use all types of cord, in particular viscose cord, the next best thing to real silk cord, but less expensive and easier to come by. This cord typically consists of a cotton core surrounded by a woven outer section that gives it its cylindrical shape. It comes in three thicknesses: fine, 1.5mm to 2mm ($^1/_{16}$in to $^3/_{32}$in), medium, 2mm to 2.5mm ($^3/_{32}$in to $^1/_{10}$in) and thick, 2.5mm ($^1/_{10}$in) and over.

When starting out, use approximately 2mm ($^3/_{32}$in) cylindrical cord in cotton or viscose as this is easiest to work with. As you progress, you can start to use thicker or thinner cord and work with all sorts of cording and ribbons, like satin cord and even soutache braid. Be careful to avoid twisting your thread when working with flat cord.

Tools

Scissors

Where possible, use a pair of dressmaking scissors to cut your cord to the desired length before making up a knot and to trim the excess close to the knot when your work is finished.

Awl

A beading or knotting awl makes it easier to pull a strand away from your knotwork. It will help you to keep your work even when you come to tighten it and, should the need arise, to undo a knot. Awls can be purchased from a specialist haberdashery. Failing this, the tip of a large tapestry needle will suffice.

Latch hook

The crochet hook shown above is known as a latch hook and is used for threading a length of cord through a tightened knot. Its latch enables you to trap the cord inside the end. This prevents you from catching other strands in your work and makes passing through a knot much easier. You can find these hooks in selected haberdasheries. If you are unable to get hold of one, use a standard crochet hook (no. 1$^1/_2$ to 2) to fit the size of your cord.

Flat-nosed pliers

Flat-nosed pliers are used for finishing jewellery, to hold small metal pieces in place when working with mounts and findings, and to open and close jump rings.

Accessories

Beads

All sorts of beads lend themselves to creating jewellery and accessories using knot craft:
- beads and discs made from natural materials like mother-of-pearl, jade and semi-precious stone;

- traditional embroidered Korean medallions;

- novelty beads such as those made from Murano glass.

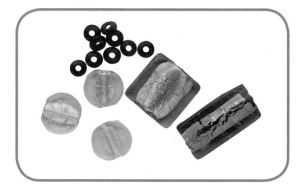

To make it easy to thread on your beads, it is important to ensure that the diameter of the hole is at least as large as that of your cord.

Mounts and findings

This category includes all the various accessories used to finish off pieces of jewellery. The following mounts and findings are used in this book: chokers, brooch mounts, earring findings, keyrings, trigger clasps and small jump rings, which are used as connectors.

9

Tips for good technique

Using your tools

Traditionally, the hands are the only tools used in Korean knot craft. Unlike Chinese knotting, the Korean knot artist works with the fingers only. To make up certain knots, however, you may find it easier to use an awl and latch hook as needed. These will give you a neater finish.

To use the hook, open the latch underneath the hook completely and insert the hook into the knot through which you want to thread your cord.

Place your cord in the tip of the hook and close the latch. Pull the hook back through the knot to thread the cord through and bring it out on the other side.

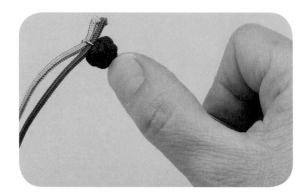

Before tying a knot, apply a little fabric glue to the ends of your cord to prevent fraying.

Starting off

In the first part of this book, each of the 11 basic knots has been made up using two threads in contrasting colours so you can see how the strands are interwoven to form each knot. Traditionally, Korean knots are made using only a single length of cord, which is halved at the start to give you two strands to work with. It is recommended that you practise using two different coloured cords, following the detailed instructions for each knot carefully. When you have become more skilled, you can try making up same-colour knots using just one cord.

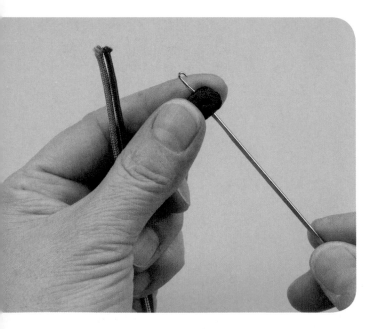

To revitalize a practice length of cord, moisten it slightly and smooth it down to restore its original shape and flexibility.

Starting knot and starting point

Two cords

When working with two lengths of cord, tie them together at one end in a basic knot or an overhand knot, or even a double connection knot (see double connection knot, page 14), that you will be able to undo easily at a later stage. This knot will mark the starting point of your work.

One cord

When working with a single length of cord halved at its centre, tie a starting knot to mark your starting point. This will serve as a point of reference while you are working. Occasionally it will be necessary to locate the middle of the cord before tying your starting knot. This will help you to keep the size of the loops in some of your motifs even when you come to tighten and finish off. To do this, start by tying a length of fine thread at the centre of the cord. Halve the cord, then tie an overhand knot in the doubled-up cord, making sure that the strands remain parallel. You can then undo this knot easily when your work is finished.

Tightening

Making a knot involves two steps: weaving and tightening. Tightening is the final stage in the process, in which a knot is modelled and shaped. It is important to use even pressure on your cord at all times when tightening, to obtain a perfectly symmetrical knot. To ensure an even finish when tightening, always work from the starting knot towards the ends of the strands, following the direction of the thread through the knot.

Knots: front and back

The motifs in Korean decorative knot craft are perfectly symmetrical. Some knots have a back and a front, like the series of knots that use the ginger or chrysanthemum motifs. On the front side, the top strand in the central pattern of the knot goes diagonally from right (top) to left (bottom). A good way to remember this is to think about travelling from a city in the north east to one in the south west.

Ginger knot: front.

Ginger knot: back.

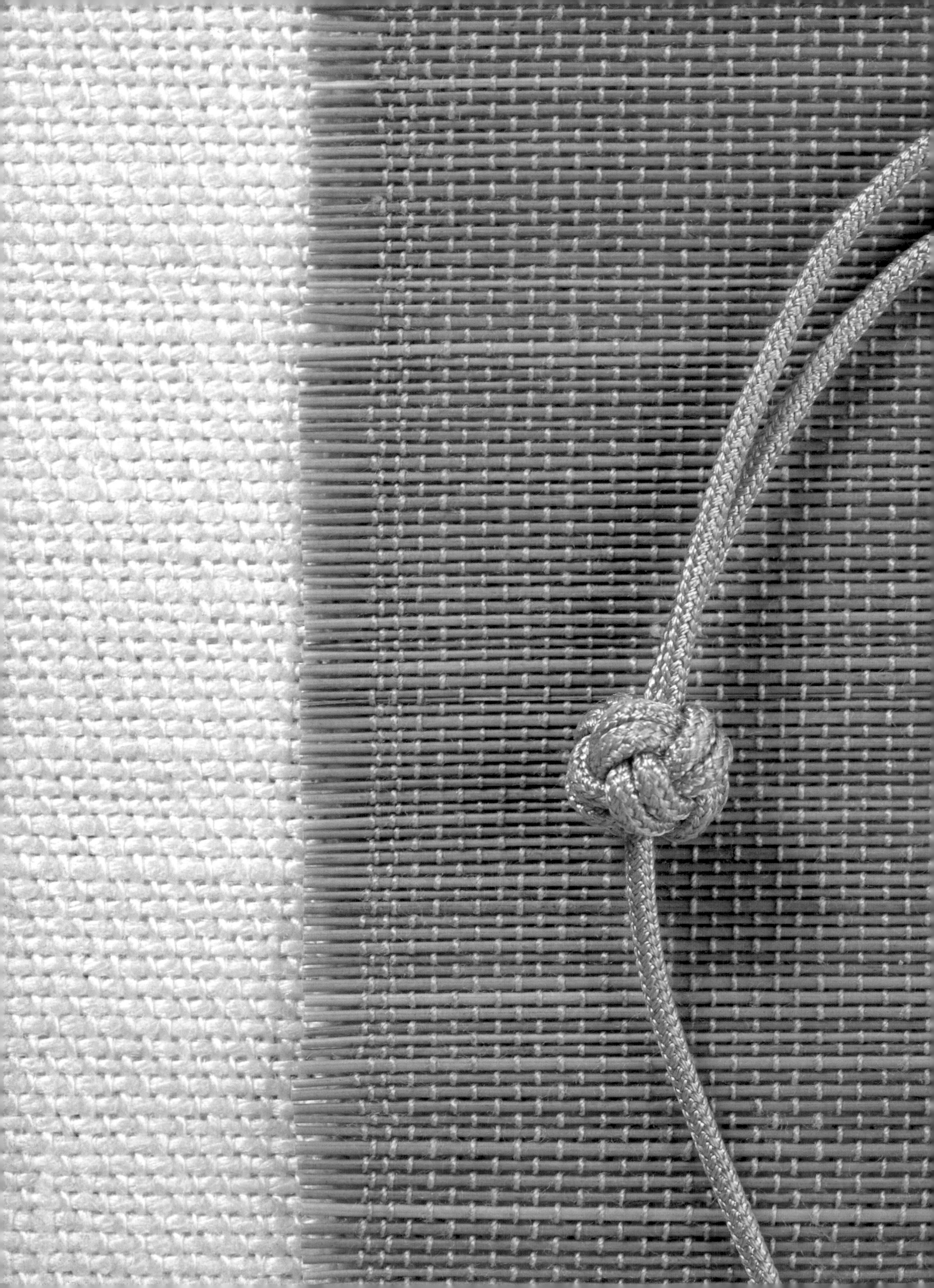

Basic knots

Double connection knot

This is considered the most straightforward of all the Korean knots. It is made from two interwoven loops and the strands that make the knot are criss-crossed in opposite directions on each side of the knot. The double connection knot is very often used for the beginning of a design.

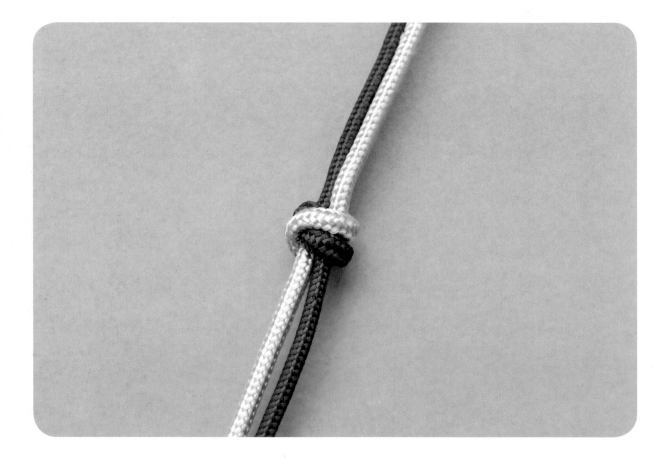

2 Wrap the lower strand around the upper strand from front to back to make a loop approximately 1cm (³/₈in) in diameter.

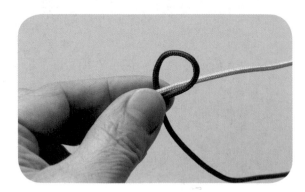

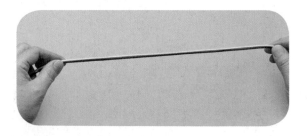

1 Use one 2m (78¹/₂in) length of cord halved, or two 1m (39¹/₄in) lengths of cord. This will give you plenty to work with should you wish to make up several knots. Hold the two strands out horizontally in front of you, ensuring that they remain parallel.

Hold the loop between your left thumb and index finger at 45 degrees to the horizontal strand. Position the end extending from the looped thread on the vertical, keeping the other strand on the horizontal as before.

3 Take the lower strand and thread it through the loop, from left to right (3a). Bring the end out of the loop, pull the strand through and secure the lower thread on top of the other strand with your left thumb, so the strands are now the opposite way round to their starting position in step 1 (3b). Use your right hand to keep the strands parallel on the horizontal.

4 Place your right thumb at the base of the loop (4a). Turn the loop 360 degrees away from you. One quarter of the way around, lift up your left index finger to allow the loop through (4b), then replace it immediately to finish the turn. When the turn is complete, place your left thumb inside the loop (4c).

4a

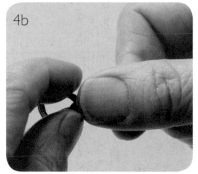

4b

3a

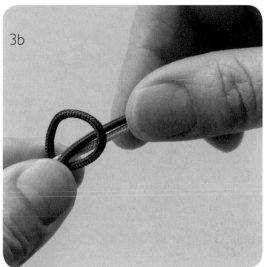

3b

4c

5 Pass the second strand (mauve) from front to back to make a second loop to the right of the first. Position the base of the second loop to the left of the base of the first loop and secure with your left index finger.

7 Pull the upper thread (blue) to tighten the first loop and lay the strands out parallel on the right again.

6 Thread the end that extends from the second loop through the two loops (6a) and place it below the strand that extends from the first loop (6b). Position the two strands so they are parallel on the horizontal.

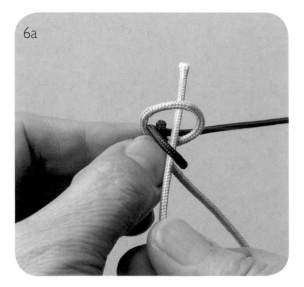

8 Using your right thumb, position the second loop so that it overlaps the first in the shape of an X (8a). Hold the second loop between your left thumb and index finger, then pull the lower strand to tighten in the same way as before (8b).

8a

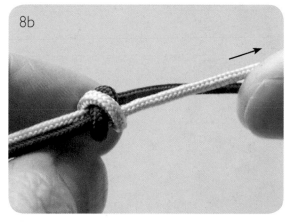

8b

Double connection knot.

Lotus knot

A symbol of purity and fertility, the lotus is one of the most revered flowers in Buddhist symbolism and features widely in Korean art. Once tightened, this knot resembles a lotus bud. Traditionally used to make buttons for clothing, it is also known as the 'button knot'.

1 Work with two 1m (39¼in) lengths of cord tied together at one end, or with one 2m (78½in) length of cord. If working with a single length, mark the middle by tying a short length of fine thread, then tie a basic knot (see page 11). Place this starting knot between your left thumb and index finger. It is a point of reference as you weave around it. Pass the left strand around the back of your thumb and bring it to the front, securing the end with your ring finger and little finger.

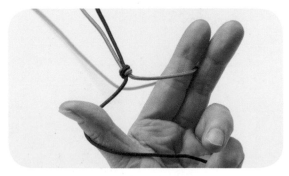

Thread the right strand from front to back between your index and middle fingers.

2 Bring the right strand (blue) round to the left, passing behind the starting knot, and bring it to the front of your hand, passing to the left of the starting knot (2a). Take the left strand (brown) towards the back of your hand, passing to the right of the starting knot and across the base of your index finger (2b).

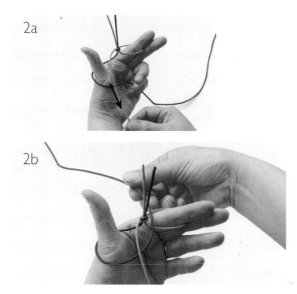

2a

2b

3 Keep working with the same end (brown). Pass it behind and then to the left of your starting knot. Thread it upwards through the loop you have made around your thumb (3a and 3b).

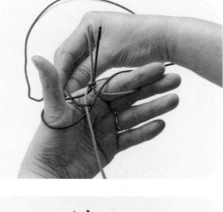

3a

3b

4 Take the other end (blue) and thread it upwards through the loop you have made around your index finger (4a and 4b).

4a

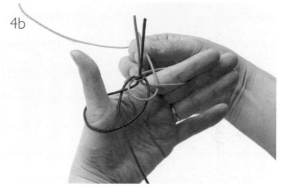

4b

5 Keep working with the same end. Go around the back of your starting knot from right to left, then thread the end downwards into the loop you made in the previous step just in front of your starting knot (5a and 5b).

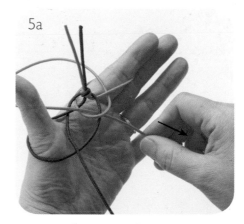

5a

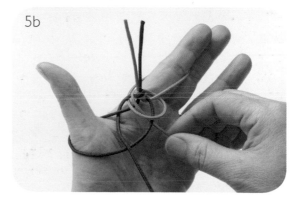

5b

6 Bring the left strand (brown) round to the right by going around the front of the starting knot, then insert it downwards just behind your starting knot (6a and 6b).

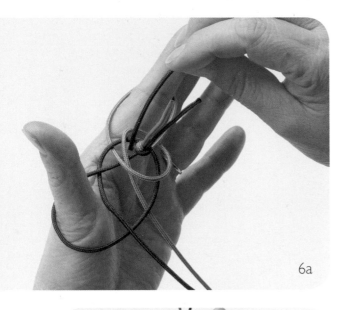

6a

6b

7 Pull each strand and the starting knot in turn to tighten your work (7a and 7b).

7a

7b

8 Take out your left thumb and index finger (8a). Hold the starting knot in your right hand and pull it gently upwards. With your left hand, gently pull your work downwards to tighten (8b and 8c).

8a

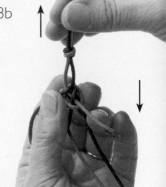

8b

8c

Tightening and adjusting

Lay your work out horizontally (9a). You should have two strands on either side of your lotus knot. If you want to move your lotus knot to the right, you need to locate the extension of each right strand in your knot. If you want to move your lotus knot to the left, locate the extension of each left strand in your knot. Work each strand one by one in turn.

9a

Final steps

Insert your awl into the extension of your first strand (shown on the right here) in your knot (9b). Pull it outwards to form a loop. This will make the first strand shorter (9c).

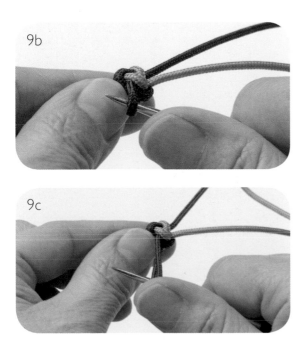

Locate the extension of the loop in your work and pull on the corresponding end to move the loop (9d and 9e). Continue to work in this way, turning the knot in the same direction every time, until you are able to tighten the loop you have made by pulling on the other end of the strand to the left of the knot (9f and 9g). Repeat with the second strand on the right.

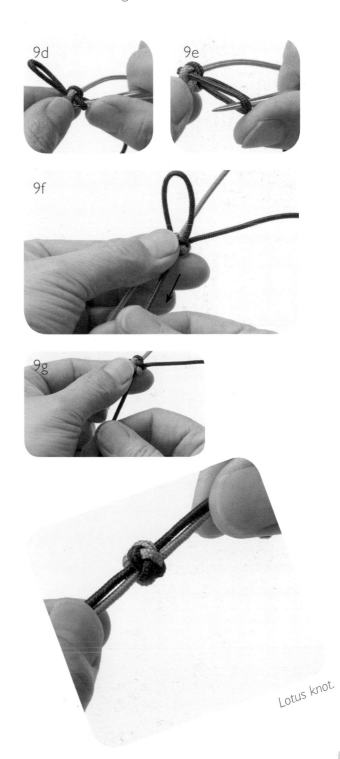

Lotus knot.

Ring knot

The ring knot takes its name from the fact that it is woven around your finger. You can make a larger motif simply by adding more units to your ring. Two versions of the ring knot are shown here, with four and five units respectively. Each version of the knot has two variants: a tight, ball-shaped knot and a flat knot. In its ball-shaped version this knot can be used as a bead.

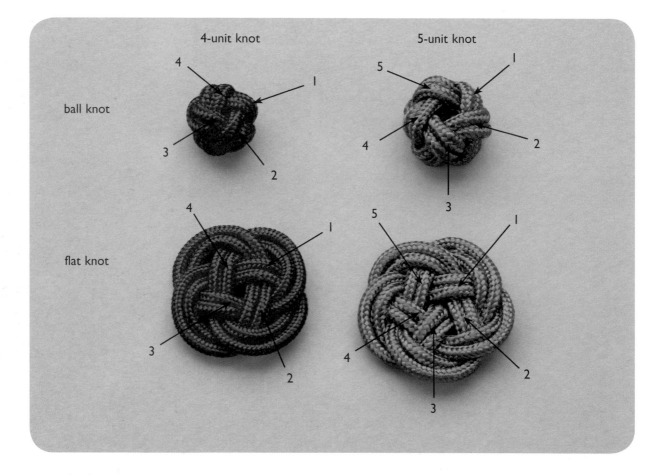

Four-unit ring knot

1 Take one 1m (39¼in) length of cord and mark your starting point at its centre. Work with about 50cm (20in) of the right end.

2 Wind the cord twice around your left index finger to make a ring and secure with your thumb.

3 Insert your awl through the right strand of the ring (3a). Lift the loop over the left strand by turning over the awl: the left strand should now be on the right (3b).

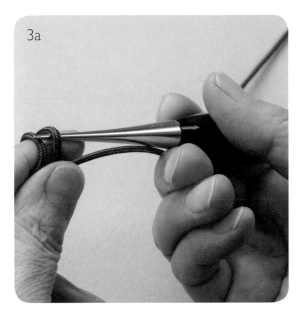
3a

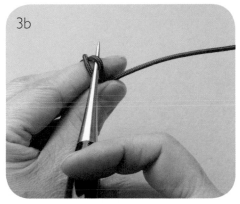
3b

4 Insert the loose end of the cord between the two strands of your ring from left to right just after the first cross made in the previous step (4a and 4b).

4a

4b

5 Turn the ring on your finger so the next cross is now facing towards you (5a).

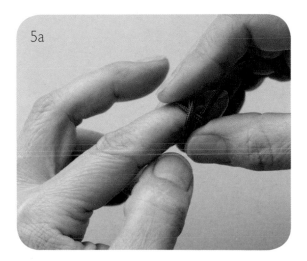
5a

Thread the end between the two strands of the ring from right to left just after this cross (5b and 5c).

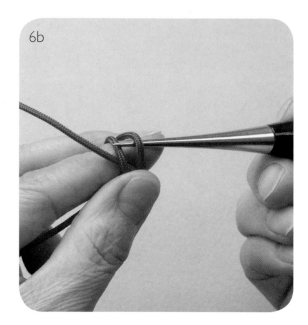

6b

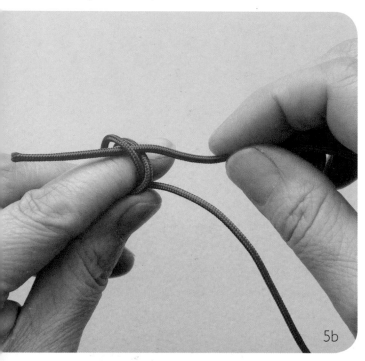

5b

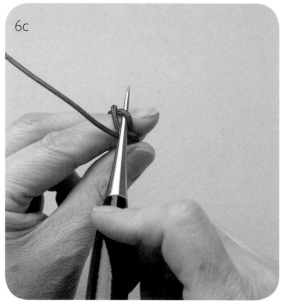

6c

5c

6 Turn the ring towards you slightly on your finger (6a). Repeat steps 3 and 4 (6b, 6c and 6d).

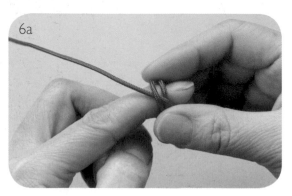

6a

6d

7 Take the ring off your finger. Position the point where the left and right strands line up in front of you and put the ring back on your finger. Lay the right strand up and to the right and the left strand down and to the left of their meeting point (7a). Continue to work only with the right loose end to double up your ring knotwork. Use your awl to help thread the end into your work (7b, 7c and 7d). Always double up your work on the right-hand side of the original strand (7e, 7f). Once you have been round three times, you will have doubled each of the three strands in your work (7g).

7d

7e

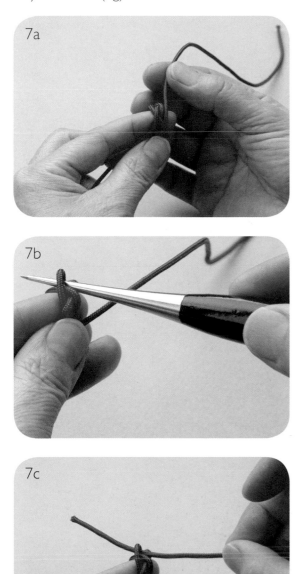

7a

7b

7c

7f

7g

Ball knot

Final steps

Using your awl, at the point where the two loose ends line up, pull the strands on the left of your work towards you (8a and 8b). Make two identical loops. Look for the extension of the strands that form these two loops in your work and pull it outwards. Move the loops all the way around the knot in this way, working in the same direction as you go (8c, 8d and 8e) until the loop on the left can be tightened by pulling the left strand (8f).

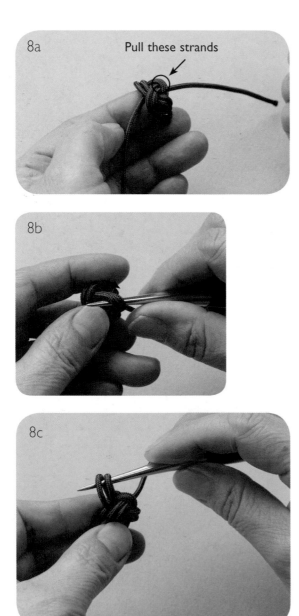

8a Pull these strands

Again using your awl, continue to follow the extension of the remaining loop in the knot (8g and 8h). Move it around your work until you are able to tighten it by pulling on one of the loose ends, in the same way as in the previous step (8i). Adjust your work by repeating this process as many times as necessary to give you a neat, circular finish.

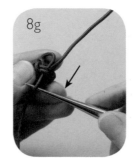

8i

Four-unit ball ring knot.

When making several ring knots in one cord, tighten and move the last knot made up to the left end of the cord before starting on the next knot using the loose end on the right. To use the knots as beads, trim the ends close to each knot.

Flat knot

Final steps

To make the flat version of the knot, at the end of step 7 fold one of the edges of the ring towards the other edge, then flatten out your work (8j and 8k). To tighten, proceed in the same way as for the ball knot but with your work laid out flat.

8j 8k

After tightening and shaping the knot, trim the two ends close up to it and secure them with a little glue on the reverse.

How to move a tightened ball ring knot

When this knot has been properly tightened it can be moved to one end of your cord. To do this you must shorten the length of the strand on this side and transfer the length to the opposite end by passing it through your knot. Locate the extension of the end you need to shorten in the knot at the point where the two strands on either side of the knot line up. Using your awl, make a loop in the extension of this strand in your knot. The end will get shorter as your loop gets longer. Insert your awl into the extension of the loop in the knot and pull it towards you. Move the loop all the way around your knot, working in the same direction all the time, until you can tighten it by pulling on the other strand.

Four-unit flat ring knot.

Five-unit ring knot

The second version of the knot has an extra crossover in its design. This is introduced at the beginning, in step 2.

1 Follow the instructions for step 1 of the four-unit ring knot on page 22.

2 Wind the cord twice around your left index finger, crossing over to the left as you go (2a, 2b and 2c). Secure the cross motif you have made with your thumb (2d).

2c

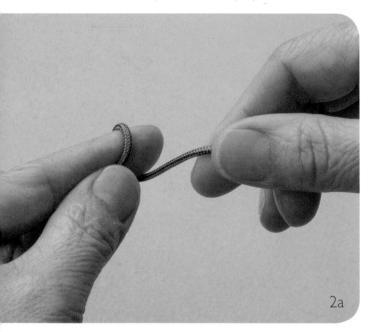

2a

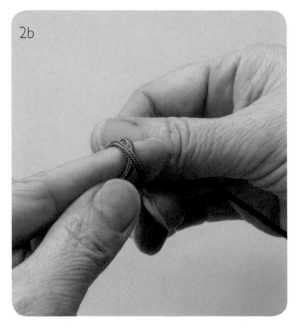

2b

2d

3 Insert your awl into the right strand above the cross in the two strands that form the ring around your index finger, and hook it over the top of the left strand by turning over the awl. The left strand should now be on the right.

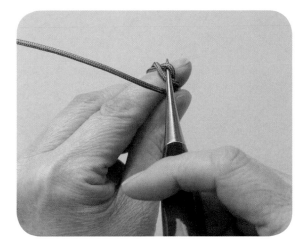

Now follow exactly the same instructions as for the four-unit ring knot, starting from step 4 on page 23.

Five-unit flat ring knot.

Five-unit ball ring knot.

Spectacle knot

This straightforward knot takes its name from an everyday object. When finished, it forms a perfect square. Make two knots up one after the other and you have what resembles a pair of glasses!

1 Work with two 1m (39¹/₄in) lengths of cord tied together at one end, or one 2m (78¹/₂in) length of cord. If working with a single length of cord, mark the middle of the cord by tying a short length of fine thread at its centre, then tie a basic knot (see page 11).

2 Lay the starting knot out in front of you. Cross the two strands by threading the right strand over the left strand and then tying them loosely (2a). Make up three other loose knots in the same way (2b).

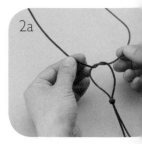

2a

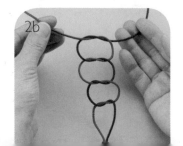

2b

3 Take the right end, bring it down to the first knot and slide it under the right strand (black) that separates the starting knot from the first knot. Thread it between the two strands that make up the first knot (3a). Thread the strand through the next three knots in the same way (3b). Once you have gone through the last knot, pull the end gently towards the top of your work, without completely tightening the loop it forms on the right (3c).

4 Take the left end and thread it over the left strand (red) between the starting knot and the first knot. Next, thread it between the strands that make up the four knots, parallel to the right strand and on its left. Once you have gone through the last knot, pull the end gently towards the top of your work, without completely tightening the loop it forms on the left. Ensure the strands of the right-hand loop go under the strands of the other knots and the strands of the left-hand loop go over the strands of the other knots.

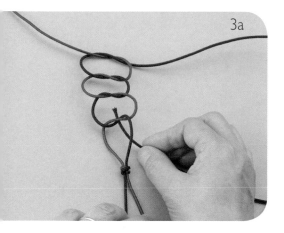

3a

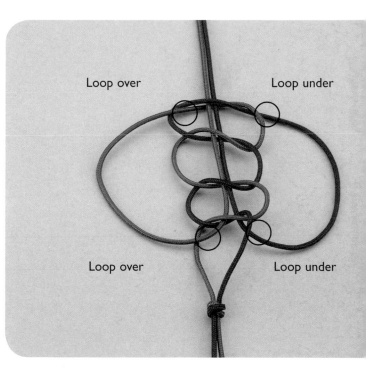

Loop over   Loop under

Loop over   Loop under

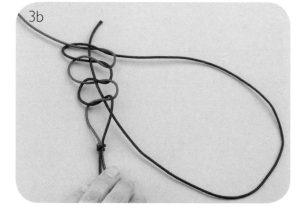

3b

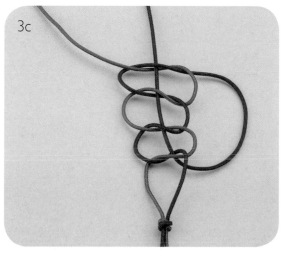

3c

5 Tighten your weaving by pulling on the loops of the four knots. Start by pulling the first pair of loops between the first and the second knot, so that the first knot moves closer to the starting knot, making sure that you leave a space the thickness of two cord widths (5a). Then tighten the next two pairs of loops (5b, 5c, 5d and 5e). To tighten the last pair of loops, pull on the loops linking the first and fourth knots (5f and 5g).

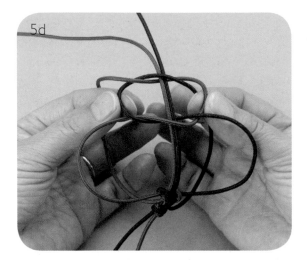

5d

5a

5e

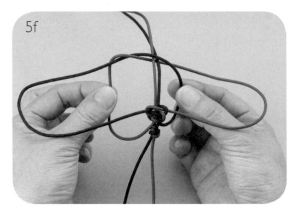

5f

5b

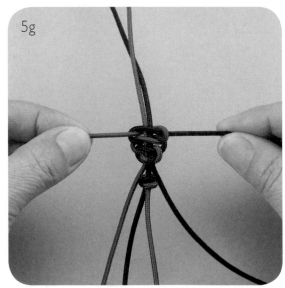

5g

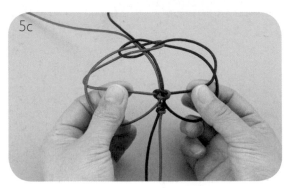

5c

6 To tighten the last two loops on either side of the knot, hold your work out horizontally with your starting knot on the left (6a). Pull the end of the upper strand to the right of the knot to make the first loop smaller, without tightening it completely (6b and 6c). Turn your work over so the remaining loop is at the top and tighten as before (6d and 6e). Ensure that you leave a little space between the starting knot and the series of four knots.

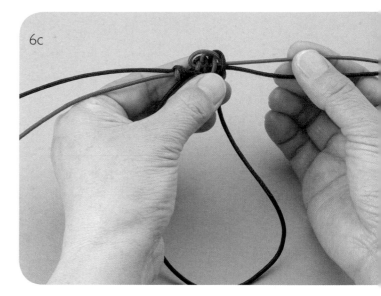

6c

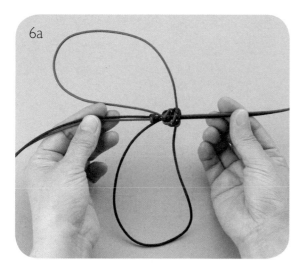

6a

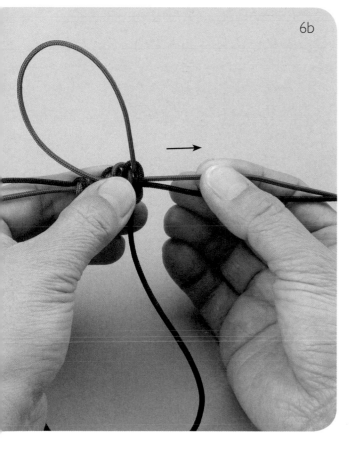

6b

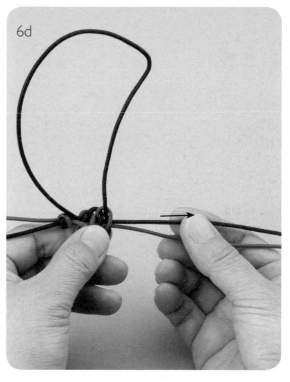

6d

6e

7 Keeping your work in front of you on the horizontal, take the back strand of the fourth knot on the right side between your right index finger and thumb (7a), take the front strand of the same knot in your left index finger and thumb (7b), and bring these two strands to the left of your work, in front of the first knot in the series (7c and 7d). Next, pull the ends of each of the strands to the right to tighten the knot (7e and 7f).

7a

7d

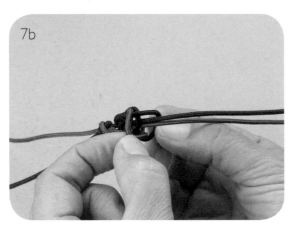

7b

7c

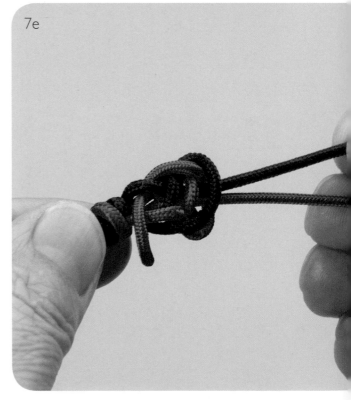

7e

7f

8 On the right, hold the back strand of the third knot between your right index finger and thumb, take the front strand of the same knot in your left index finger and thumb (8a), and bring these two strands to the left of your work and to the left of the fourth knot you have already pulled over (8b and 8c).

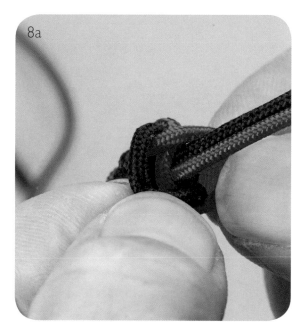

8a

8b

9 Finishing & shaping

To adjust your spectacle knot, use your awl to pull the strand in the knot that corresponds to the extension of the strand you want to shorten. This will create a loop. Move the loop around your work, following the extension of the strand and working in the same direction – towards the end of the strand – all the time. Continue to work in this way until the excess length has disappeared when you pull the end of the strand. Repeat this process with each of the strands if necessary, until the motif looks even.

8c

Spectacle knot.

Dragonfly knot

This knot is made using a combination of three different knots. The dragonfly's body is made from a series of double connection knots (see page 14). A lotus knot (see page 18) forms the head. Each of the two sets of dragonfly wings is an extension of a knot in the central square motif. In Korea, the dragonfly is a symbol of victory.

1 Work with two 1m (39¼in) lengths of cord, beginning 10cm (4in) from the left end. You can also use one halved 2m (78½in) length of cord and begin from the fold that marks its centre. First, make up five double connection knots (see page 14) in succession to form the body of the dragonfly (1a and 1b).

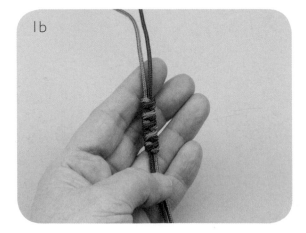

2 Hold the five double connection knots out vertically in front of you. Cross the two ends, passing the right strand over the left strand (2a), then tie them in a simple knot without tightening the knot completely (2b and 2c).

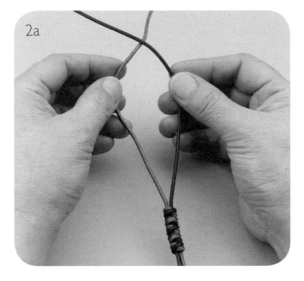

2a

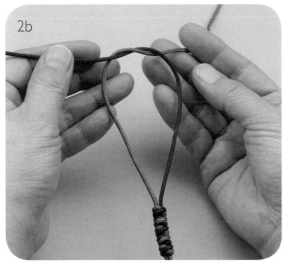

2b

2c

3 Now make up your first pair of dragonfly wings. Bend the right strand (green) back on itself and over to the left, passing it behind the strands at the base of the knot you made in step 2, to form a loop 3cm (1in) in length (3a). Bend the left strand (red) back on itself and over to the right, passing it around the front, to form a matching loop (3b).

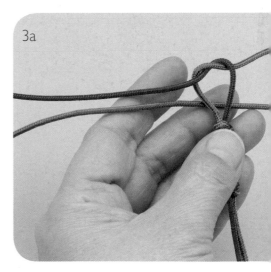

3a

3b

4 Hold all the strands firmly at the base of the wings between your left thumb and index finger. Thread the right strand (red) around the back of the right wing (green), then thread it upwards through the centre of the knot (4a and 4b). Thread the left strand (green) around the front of the left wing (red) and pass it upwards through the centre of the knot (4c and 4d).

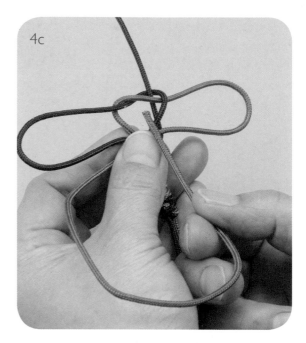

4c

4a

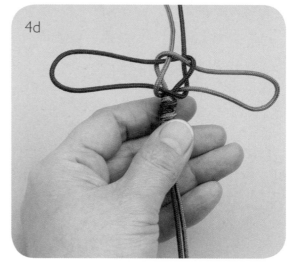

4d

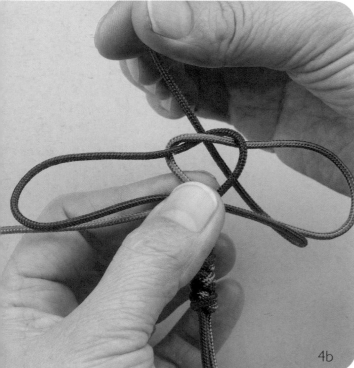

4b

5 Tighten the centre knot by gently pulling the wings (5a).

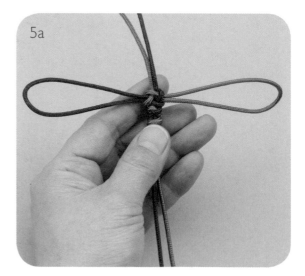

5a

Now adjust the lengths of the wings to 3cm (1in). To adjust the left wing (red), insert your awl into the strand (red) in the bottom right of the centre knot (5b). To shorten the wing, pull the strand in the bottom right of the centre knot towards the right, adjust the wing to the correct length (5c), then pull the end of the strand above the wing to tighten the centre knot (5d). To lengthen the wing, take a little length from the end above the knot, then pull the lower strand of the wing.

To lengthen or shorten the right wing (green), proceed in the same way as for the first wing, working with the bottom left strand of the centre knot (green) and the end of the strand (5e, 5f and 5g).

5b

5c

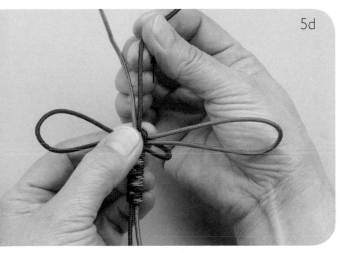

5d

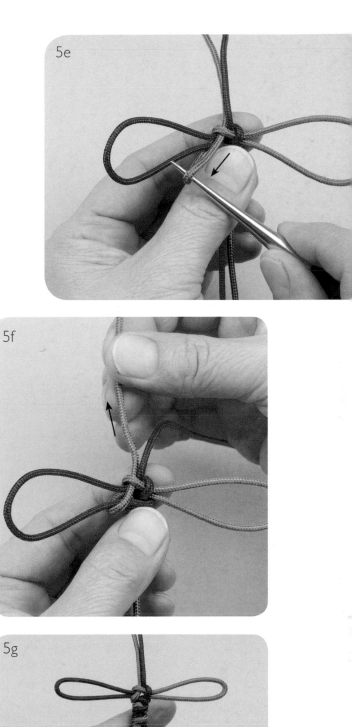

5e

5f

5g

6 Lay your work out vertically in front of you and repeat steps 2 to 5 (6a, 6b, 6c and 6d) to make the second pair of wings, this time slightly longer than the first (3.5cm or 1³/₈in) (6e and 6f).

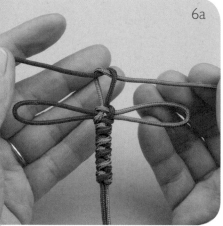

6a

6b

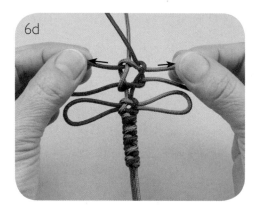

6d

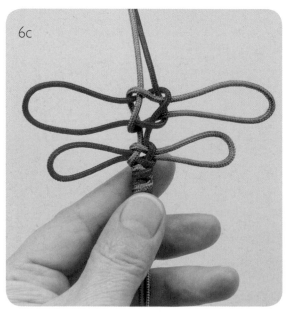

6c

6e

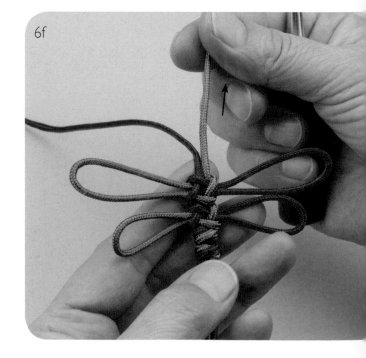

6f

7 To make the head of the dragonfly, make up a lotus knot (see page 18). Start by turning over your dragonfly so the loose ends are hanging downwards. The dragonfly's body will act as your starting knot (7a). Once complete, move the lotus knot along the cord using your awl to fix the head to the body of the dragonfly (see step 9, page 21) (7b, 7c, 7d, 7e, 7f and 7g).

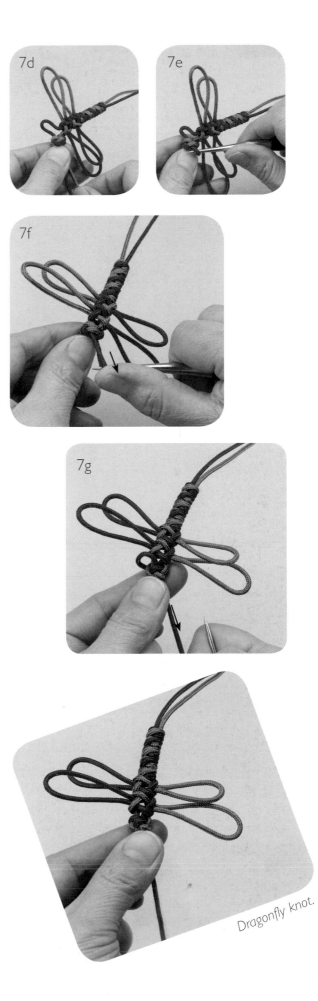

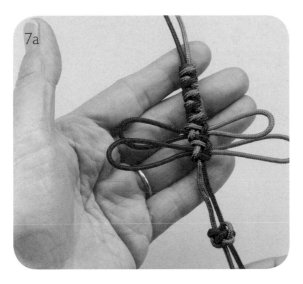

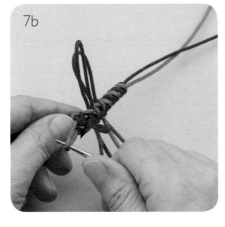

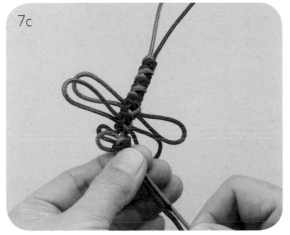

Dragonfly knot.

5 Let go of the base of the second right loop and insert your right index finger and then your thumb into the top of that loop (5a and 5b). Pick up the two strands of the left loop and thread them into the second right loop (5c).

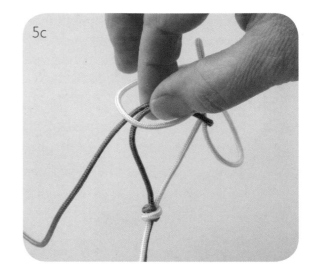

5c

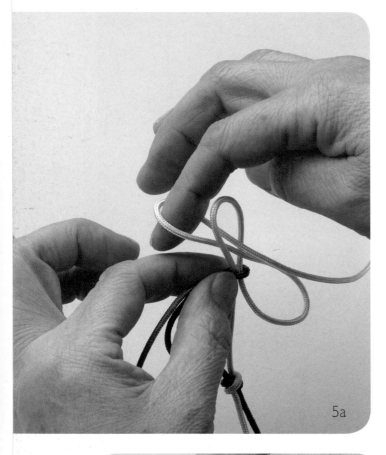

5a

6 Take the end of the left strand and pass it under the two strands in your left loop from back to front, without pulling it through completely – leave approximately 10cm (4in) (6a). Next, fold the strand back on itself, passing it over the top of the two strands of the first left loop to form a second left loop identical to the first. Hold this new loop halfway up, between your left thumb and index finger (6b).

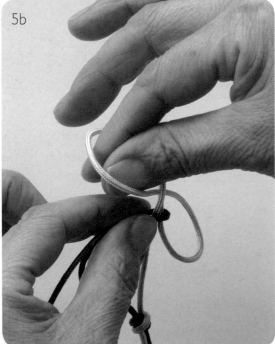

5b

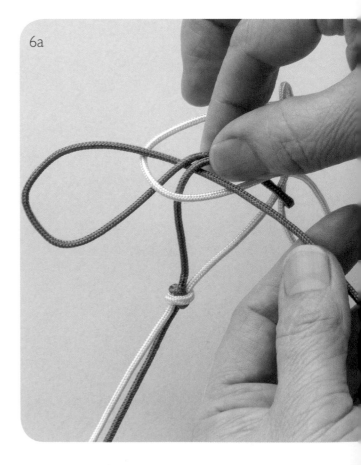

6a

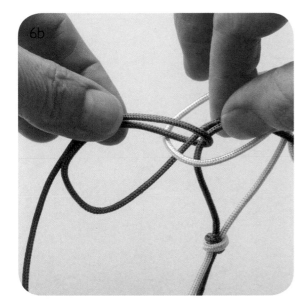

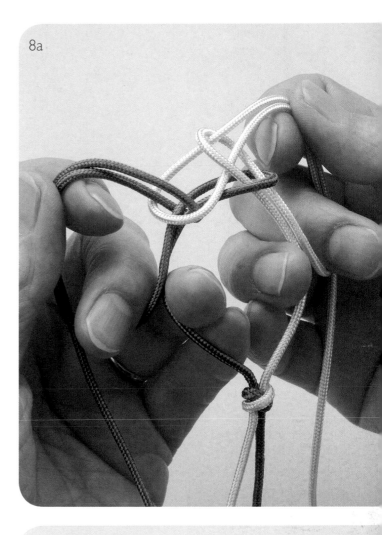

7 Move your right hand. Hold the base of the second right loop between your right thumb and index finger and lift it up gently.

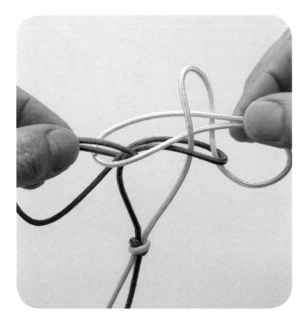

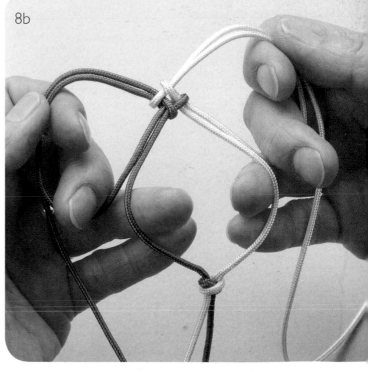

8 Place the ring finger and little finger of each hand between the two strands located just above the starting knot (8a). Pull the strands from the first right and left loops downwards, securing them between the middle finger and ring finger of each hand. Pull the strands from the second left and right loops upwards, securing them between the index finger and thumb of each hand. Pull the strands at the four corners of the knot away from each other to form the centre diamond (8b).

Strawberry Knot

This is made using three traditional knots: the ginger knot (see page 42), the wing knot from the butterfly knot (see page 80), and the ring knot (see page 22) in the centre.

1 Work using two 1m (39¼in) lengths of cord tied together at one end, or with one 2m (78½in) length of cord. If using a single length, mark the middle of the cord by tying a short length of fine thread in its centre, then tie a basic knot (see page 11).

2 Make up a ginger knot (see page 42, steps 1 to 8). Lay the knot out with the back facing you and locate the strands you need to pull (2a).

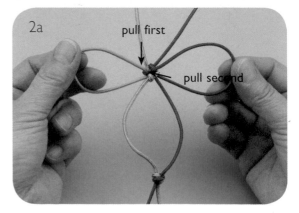

2a   pull first   pull second

Insert your awl into the strand (dark pink) in the top right of the centre diamond of the ginger knot and pull it out (2b). Pull it upwards until your starting knot is next to your centre diamond (2c and 2d). Next, pull on the lower strand of the right loop to tighten the knot (2e). You should now have a large loop on the right. Work in the same way to obtain a matching loop on the left. First pull on the strand (pale pink) in the bottom right of the centre diamond of the ginger knot, then pull on the lower strand of the left loop.

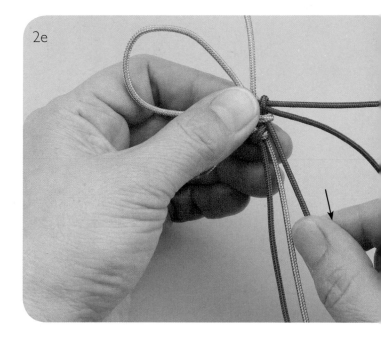

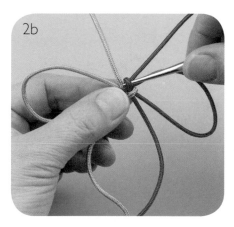

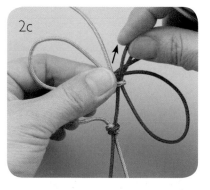

3 Make up a four-unit ring knot using another length of cord (see page 22, steps 1 to 7). Tighten it into a ball shape (see page 26, step 8, ball finish). Trim the strands on each side of the knot and hide them inside the knot. Insert your hook into the ball (3a). Pick up the two ends of the ginger knot you have just made in the end of your hook. Hold the ring knot at the end of the hook while you pull the strands towards you through the ring knot (3b).

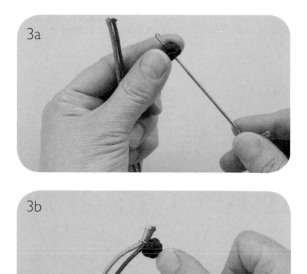

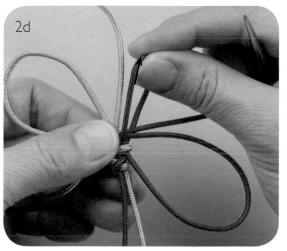

Next, slide the ring knot along the strands of cord until it sits on top of the ginger knot (3c).

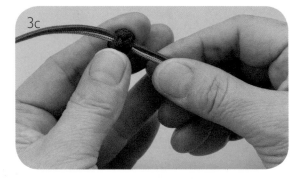

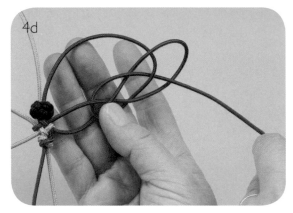

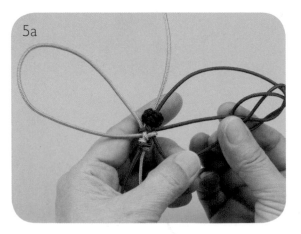

4 Continue working with the back of the ginger knot facing you. Twist the right-hand loop to form a figure of eight with the lower strand crossing over the upper strand (4a). Take the loose end (in the same colour as the loop) at the top of the ginger knot. Pass it downwards behind the outer end of the figure of eight. Bring it to the front and thread it through the first loop in the figure of eight, over the lower strand and under the upper strand (4b). With the same end, go into the second loop in the figure of eight, passing in front of the loop strand. Thread it under the strand lying vertically behind the end of the figure of eight, then bring it to the front, passing in front of the loop strand again (4c and 4d).

5 Tighten the work you did in the previous step by holding the knot in its centre and pulling on the four corner strands (5a and 5b). You should now have a wing knot. Now ensure that the strand between the top of your ring knot and the end of your wing knot is at least 14cm (5¹/₂in) in length. To make the strand longer, take as much cord as you need from the end at the bottom right of the wing knot. Next, pull the strand in the top right to lengthen the strand and tighten the knot (5c).

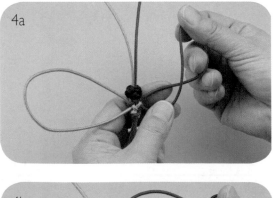

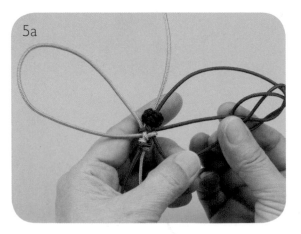

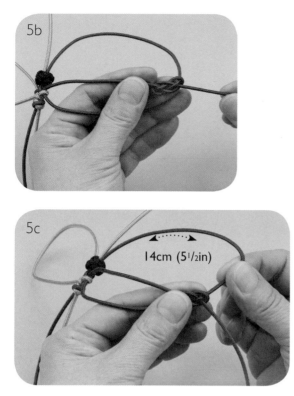

5b

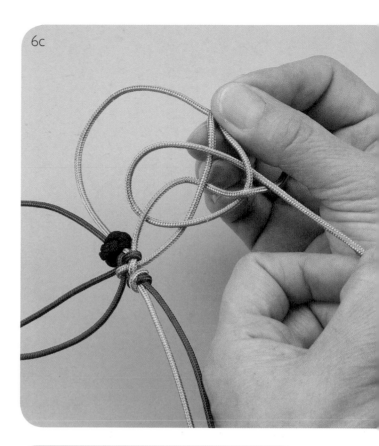

6c

5c

14cm (5¹/₂in)

6 Turn the knot over and work with the right side of the ginger knot facing you (6a). Repeat steps 4 and 5 to make a second wing knot from the left loop (6b, 6c, 6d and 6e).

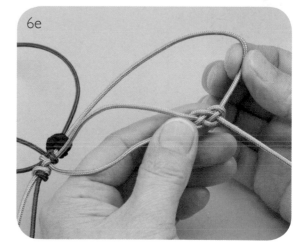

6d

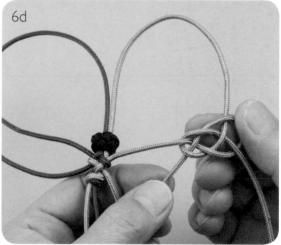

6a

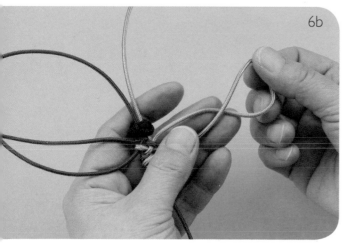

6b

6e

7 Turn your work over again so the back of the ginger knot is now facing you (7a). Tie a second ginger knot above your ring knot. Make two loops with the strands that extend from the ring knot. Hold them halfway up (7b). Thread the right loop through the left loop (7c and 7d). Make an identical loop to your first right loop using the end on the right on the far side of your wing knot (7e).

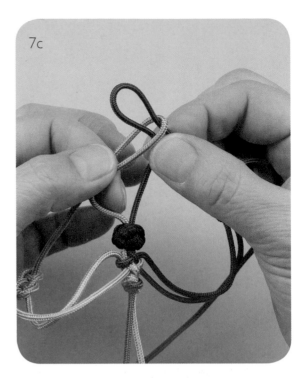

7c

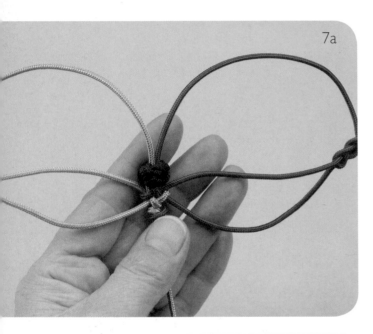

7a

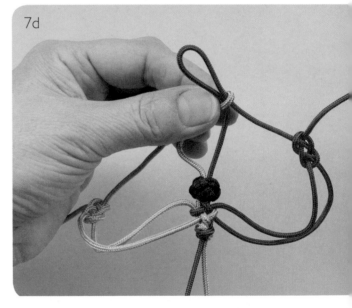

7d

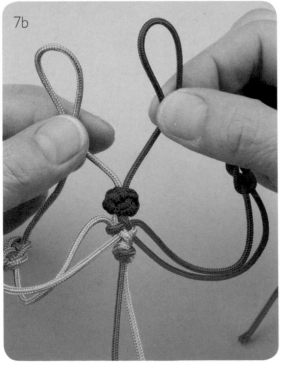

7b

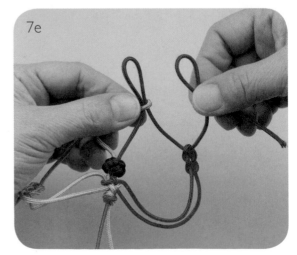

7e

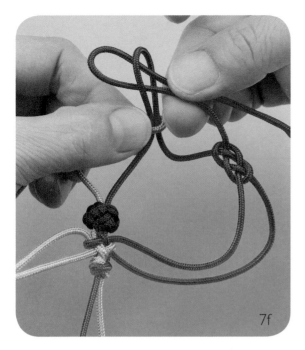

7f

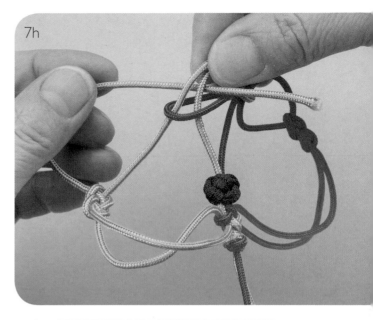

7h

Thread this loop into the first right loop (7f). Let go of the base of the second right loop. Place your right index finger and thumb through the top of the loop (7g). Pick up the two strands of the first left loop and bring them through the second right loop. Next, thread the loose end on the left on the far side of the wing knot under the two strands of the first left loop from back to front (7h) and make a second left loop to match the first by bending the strand back on itself (7i).

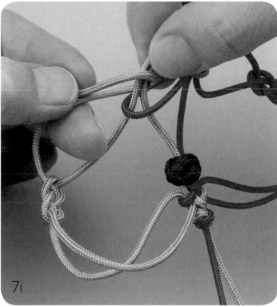

7i

Pull the strands around the knot to tighten it (7j).

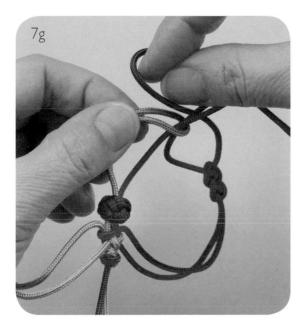

7g

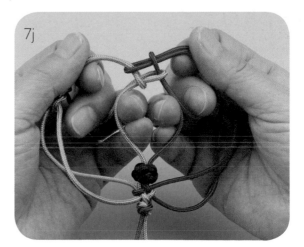

7j

8 Finishing & shaping

Tightening and adjusting

Follow the direction of your weaving (from the starting knot towards the ends of the cord) as indicated by the numbered arrows. Always adjust one side of your work and then the other, following the direction of the weave on the front and back of your work. Before tightening and adjusting your work, turn it over lengthways and widthways so your starting knot is at the top and the two ginger knots are on the reverse (8a).

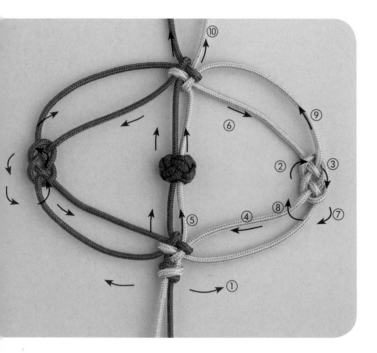

Direction of the weave: front.

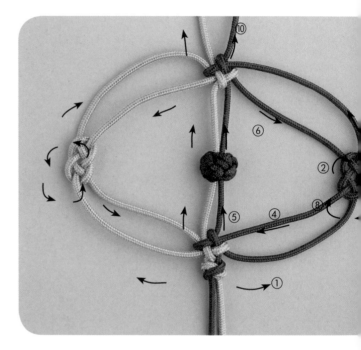

Direction of the weave: back.

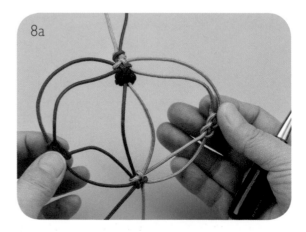

Tightening the top of your motif

To tighten the top of your motif, you need to bring the two wing knots towards the ginger knot located under the starting knot. Start by inserting your awl into the strand on the lower right of the wing knot (8b). Follow the direction of the weave through the wing knot and then through the ginger knot to transfer the excess length to the two centre strands that support the ring knot. Do the same with the second wing knot on the opposite side. Before tightening the bottom of the motif, ensure your ring knot is positioned snugly under the ginger knot and the starting knot (8c).

In your ginger knot motif, locate the extension of one of the two strands that support the ring knot. Using your awl (8d), lift up the strand and work in the direction of the weave in the wing knot, then back through the ginger knot, until all the strands are tightened when you pull the end of the strand (8e). Repeat this process with the other strand.

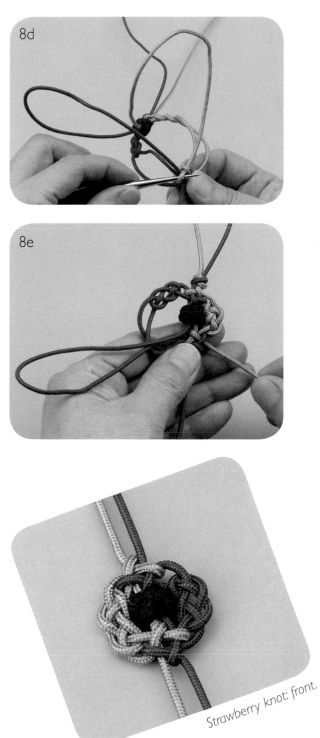

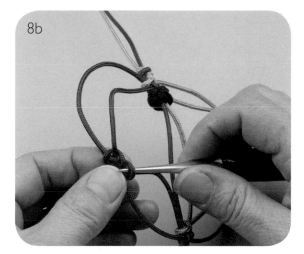

Strawberry knot: front.

Tightening the bottom of your motif

To tighten the bottom of your motif you need to remove excess cord from the two strands extending from the base of the ring knot and the strands between the two wing knots and the ginger knot at the bottom.

Plum blossom knot

The centre motif of this knot comprises six interwoven strands laid out in a star shape. Surrounding them are five loops, representing the petals of the plum blossom. Traditionally the petals are said to represent positive concepts such as long life, health, happiness, prosperity, and the life's natural journey. If another knot is tied before the plum blossom, it has only four loops.

1 Work using two 1m (39¼in) lengths of cord, tied together at one end, or with one 2m (78½in) length of cord. If using a single length of cord, mark the middle by tying a short length of fine thread in the centre, then tie a basic knot (see page 11). Place your starting knot in the

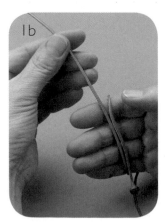

base of your right palm. Place the right strand (royal blue) behind your hand. Place the left strand (turquoise) in front of it, then wrap it once around your hand (1a and 1b).

2 Place your left index finger into the bottom of the vertical loop you have made around your right hand (loop 1). Next, while you remove your right hand from the loop, grasp the loop at the base between your left thumb and index finger.

3 Hold the right strand (royal blue) between your left index finger and middle finger, and bring it round to the right. Make a loop from about 20cm (8in) of cord. Bring the strand back to the starting point of the loop, thread it over the first strand in the loop and secure it between your left index finger and middle finger. Allow the strand extending from this loop (loop 2) to drape over the back of your hand.

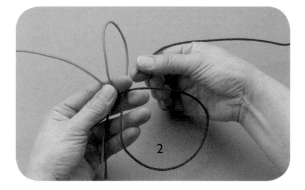

4 Take the back strand of loop 2 (4a) and bring it to the front of loop 1. Wrap it around loop 1, going around the front of your index finger (4b), then back between your middle finger and index finger (4c). You now have a new loop. Loop 3 is made from loop 2 and surrounds loop 1.

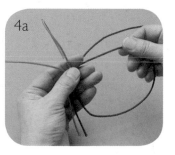

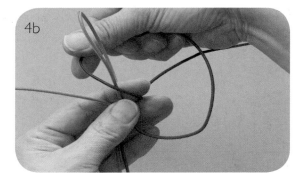

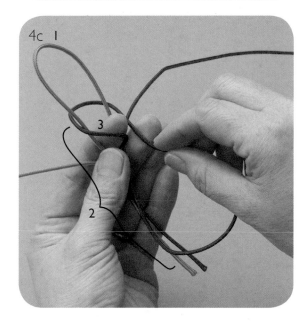

5 Now take the front strand of loop 2 and cross it over the back strand (5a). Place the cross you have made between your index finger and middle finger (5b), and secure with your thumb.

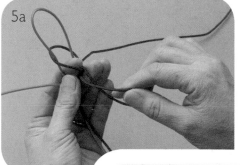

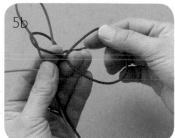

Cross the front strand of loop 2 under the back strand of loop 2. You will now have two new loops: the first around your left middle finger (loop 4) and the second after the cross (loop 5) (6a). Thread loop 1 into loop 5 (6b). Slide loop 5 under loop 3, which already contains loop 1. Bring the back strand of loop 5 to the right of loop 1, between your index finger and middle finger (6c). Make a final cross by threading the front strand over the back strand and place your middle finger in the loop you have made (loop 6) to secure (6d). Gently pull the end extending from this set of loops to tighten loop 6 (6e).

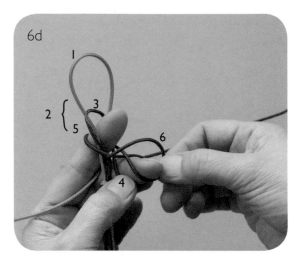

6d

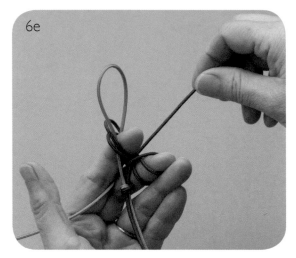

6e

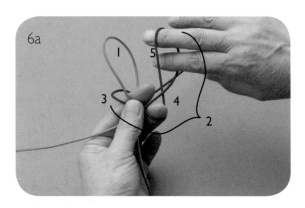

6a

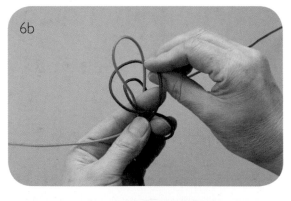

6b

Take the end (turquoise) that extends from loop 1 and thread it into loops 3 and 1 from left to right (7a). Pass it behind the other end (royal blue) (7b) and thread it into loop 6 from back to front (7c). Thread it between your index finger and middle finger (7d). Grasp it between your index finger and thumb and then thread it through loop 1 and loop 3 from right to left, passing in front of your index finger. Pull the strand gently (7e and 7f).

6c

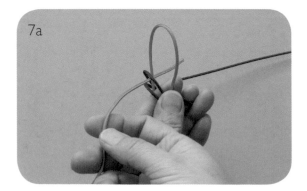

7a

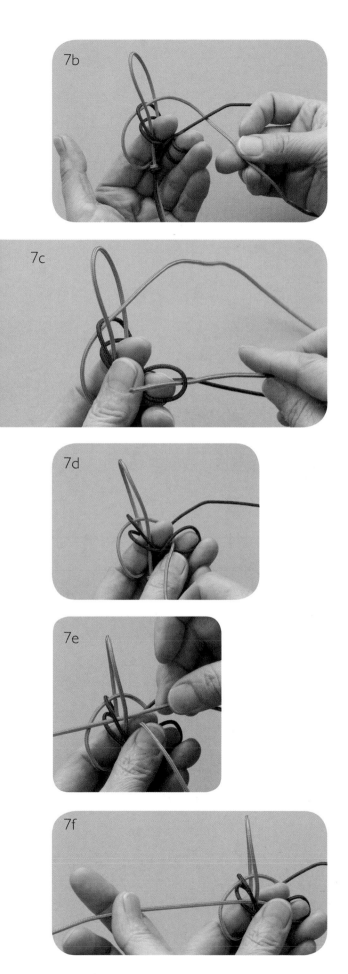

8 Continue working with the same strand (turquoise). Thread it into loop 1 from left to right (8a) and pass it behind the other end (royal blue) (8b). Next, thread it through the loop (turquoise) made by the strand itself around your index finger in step 7 (8c). Gently pull the strand downwards (8d).

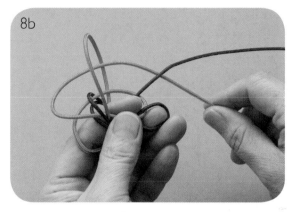

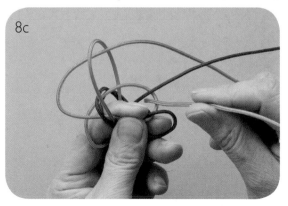

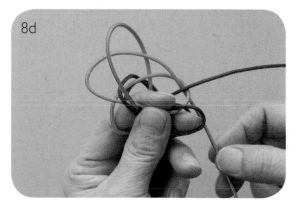

Remove your middle finger from loop 6 (8e). Thread the end into loop 4, which is still on your middle finger, from back to front, and pull downwards (8f and 8g). To finish off, thread the end upwards into the loop it made around your index finger in step 7 and into loop 1 (both made with the same strand, – here turquoise) (8h).

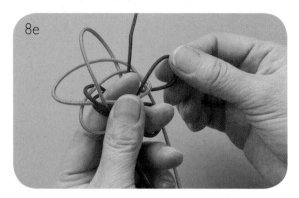

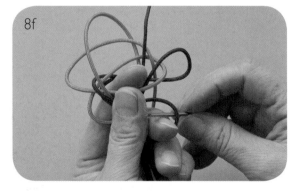

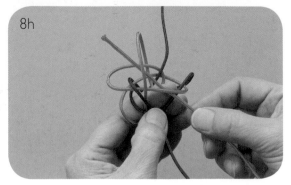

9 Pull the left end (turquoise) upwards (9a), then take out your fingers. Locate the two right loops that were on your left middle finger and pull them so the two left loops appear (9b). To tighten the loop at the top, pull the lower left loop (9c). Next, using both hands, hold each of the two large loops on either side and pull to tighten. Do the same with the strands at the top and bottom of the knot to tighten the centre (9d).

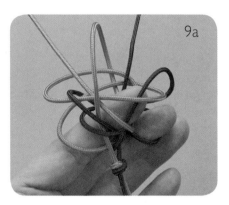

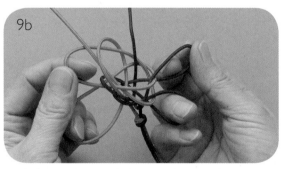

Tightening and adjusting

There are now two large loops on either side of your work. The centre motif comprises six interwoven strands laid out in a star shape. The two left loops extend from the three strands on the right of the centre motif, and vice versa. To adjust the length of the loops all the way around the plum blossom knot, locate the direction of the weave on both sides, from the starting knot to the end of the cord, for each strand. Neaten up one side of your work then the other, working with one strand first and then another.

Final steps

Turn your work over lengthways and then widthways. Your starting knot should now be at the top. To adjust the length of the two loops on the left, locate the direction of the weave through the three strands to the right of the centre motif. Start by tightening the strand that separates the plum blossom knot from the starting knot. To do this, insert your awl into the third strand in the lower left of the centre motif and pull it towards you (10a). This will create a loop. Move the loop around your work by following the direction of the weave through the centre motif of the plum blossom on the front and back, adjusting the length of the two loops one by one (10b to 10f). Repeat the process on the other side.

10c

10d

10e

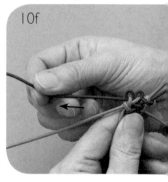

10f

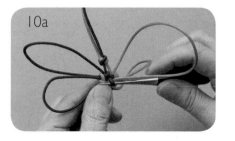

10a

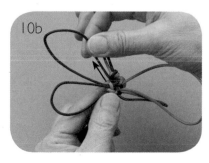

10b

Plum blossom knot: front.

Chrysanthemum knot

This knot is the traditional emblem of Korean knot craft. The chrysanthemum is a popular symbol in Korean literature, representing autumn and eternity. Four parallel lines on the right and left are interwoven in a visible weave on both sides to create a diamond-shaped motif framed by six or seven loops, depending on whether the knot is preceded by another knot.

1 Work with two 1m (39¼in) lengths of cord, tied together at one end, or with a single 2m (78½in) length. If using one length of cord, mark the middle by tying a short length of fine thread in the centre, then tie a basic knot (see page 11). Place your starting knot at the base of your right palm. Pass the right strand (plum) behind your hand. Place the left strand (mauve) in front of your hand and wrap it around your hand twice (1a and 1b).

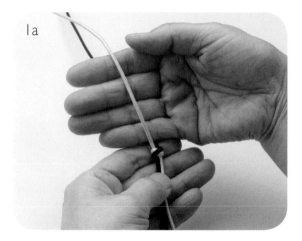

1a

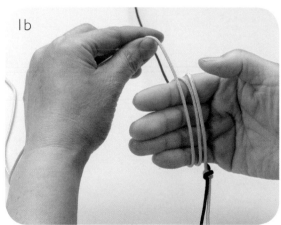

1b

2 Insert your left index finger into the bottom of the two vertical loops you have made around your right hand (2a).

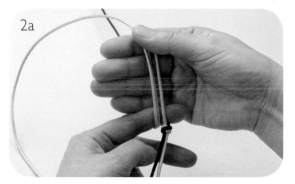

2a

Next, as you remove your right hand, hold the loops together at the bottom between your left thumb and index finger (loop 1 on the right, and loop 2 on the left) (2b).

2b

3 Bring the back strand (plum) to the right of your left hand and back to its starting point, passing it between your left index finger and middle finger, to form a third loop that is twice the size of your first two loops. Secure the strand between your left index finger and middle finger, passing it over the first strand in the loop. Leave the end extending from loop 3 hanging towards the back of your work.

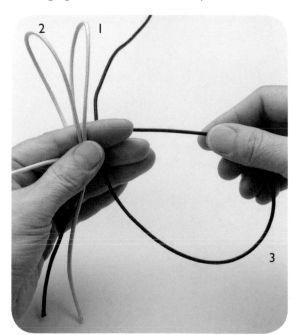

4 Take the back strand of loop 3 and bring it to the front of loops 1 and 2 and in front of your left index finger (4a). Place the strand horizontally around the two loops, then bring it to the front between your index finger and middle finger (4b and 4c). Now take the front strand of loop 3 and cross it over the back strand. Secure the cross you have made between your left index finger and middle finger. You have now made two new loops from loop 3: loop 4, which goes around loops 1 and 2, and loop 5, after the last cross you made (4d and 4e).

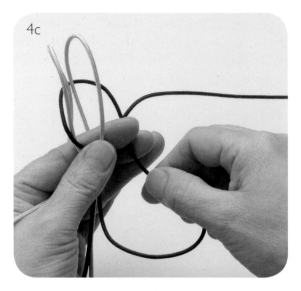

4c

4a

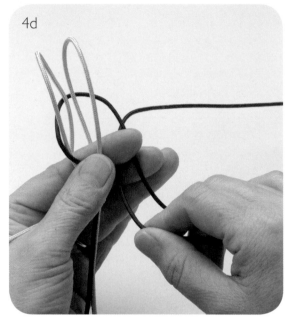

4d

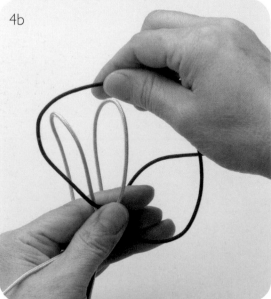

4b

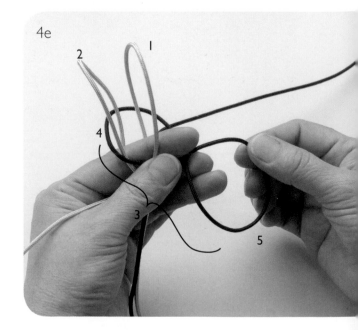

4e

5 Take the left strand (mauve) that extends from loops 1 and 2 and thread it through these two loops from left to right (5a). Pass the cord under the other end (5b), then into loop 5 from back to front, keeping it relatively loose (5c). Grasp the cord at the base of loop 5 between your left index finger and middle finger (5d). Next, take the strand over to the left and thread it through loops 1 and 2 from right to left (5e). Pull the strand through gently, passing it in front of your left index finger, and secure with your thumb (5f).

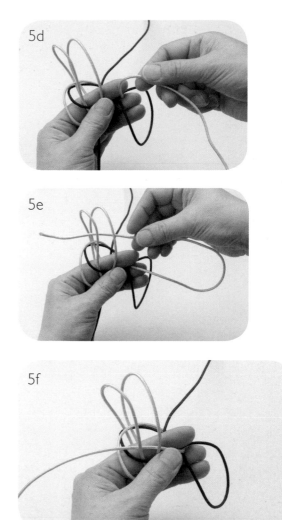

5d

5e

5f

5a

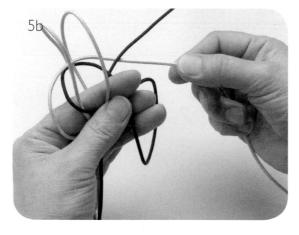

5b

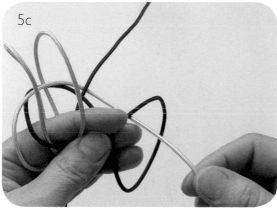

5c

6 Take the back strand of loop 5 and bring it to the front to undo the cross at the base of the loop (6a and 6b).

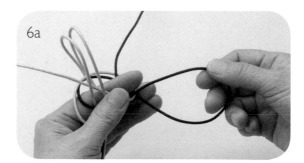

6a

6b

Next, pick up the back strand of the loop again and repeat step 4 (6c, 6d, 6e and 6f). This will give you two new loops: loop 6, the second loop surrounding loops 1 and 2, and loop 7, after the last cross you made.

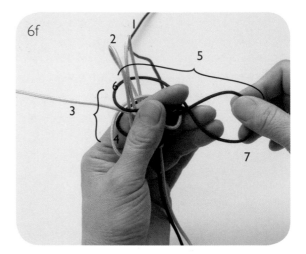

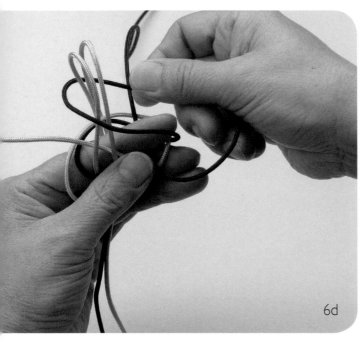

7 Take the left strand (mauve) and repeat step 5: thread it into loops 1 and 2 from left to right (7a). Pass it behind the other end (plum) (7b) and then through loop 7 from back to front (7c).

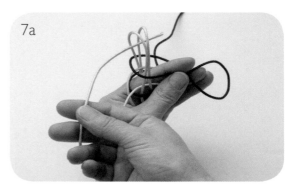

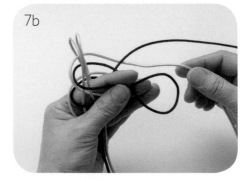

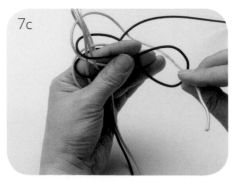

Secure it at the base of this loop between your left index finger and middle finger (7d). Next, bring the end of the strand over to the left and insert it into loops 1 and 2 from right to left (7e). Pull the strand gently, threading it in front of your left index finger, and secure it with your thumb (7f).

8 Turn your left hand 90 degrees so loop 7 is at the bottom of your work and loops 1 and 2 are horizontal (8a). Spread them out, take the end from the back (plum) and weave horizontally from right to left, passing behind, in front, behind and in front of the four vertical strands located between loops 1 and 2 (8b and 8c). Next, thread the strand into loop 2 at its base (8d). Pull gently on the strand and remove your left hand.

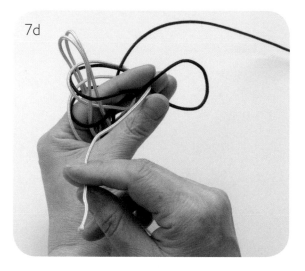

7d

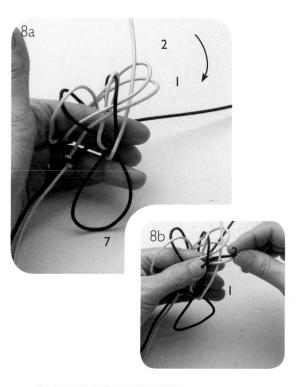

8a

8b

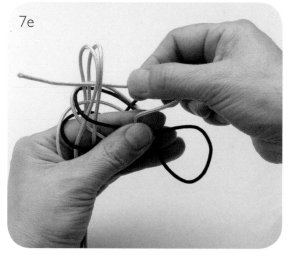

7e

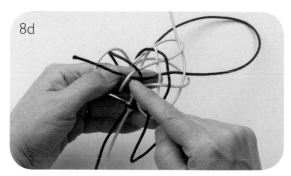

8c

8d

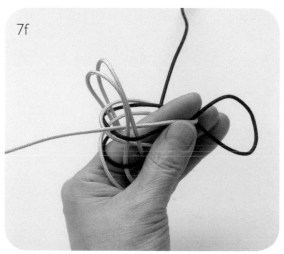

7f

9 Turn your work over widthways so the strand you are working with (plum) is on the right (9a and 9b). Place your index finger between loops 1 and 2 (9c), then weave horizontally from right to left, passing in front, behind, in front and finally behind the four vertical strands located between loops 1 and 2. Pull gently on the strand (9d).

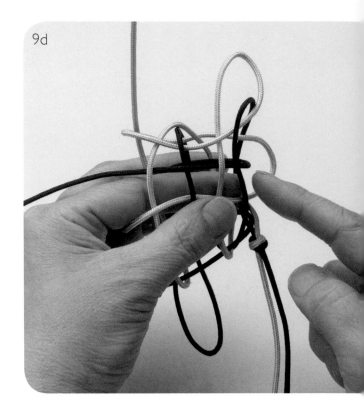

9d

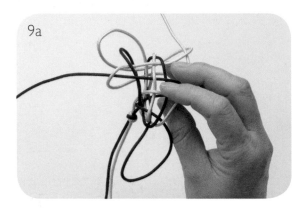

9a

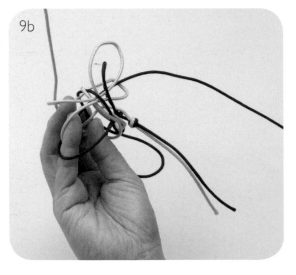

9b

10 Now form six loops all the way around your central weaving. Make the first loop on the right, just above your starting knot (10a). Next, pull on the second loop just above the first (10b). Lastly, pull on the third loop on the left of the previous loop (10c). Take out your left hand, then place the fingers of your right hand into these first three loops and pull them outwards, creating three other symmetrical loops as you go (10d).

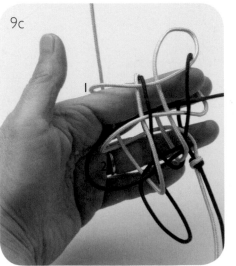

9c

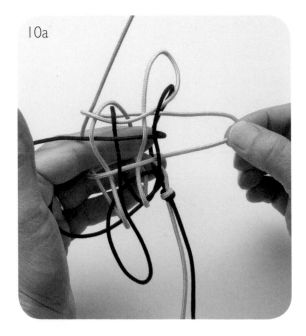

10a

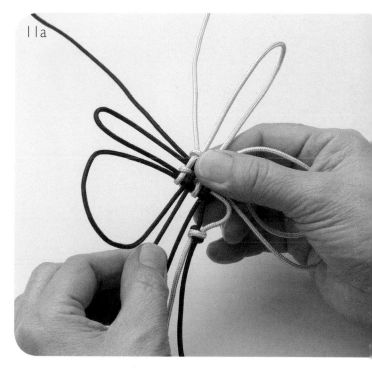

10b

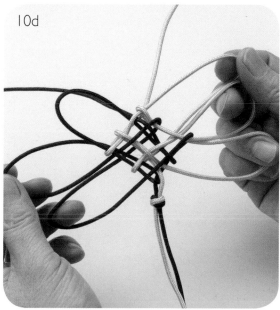

11 Next, pull the strands of each of the six loops outwards, ensuring that you maintain the diamond shape of the centre motif (11a). Even out your tightening little by little on both sides of the motif (11b).

10c

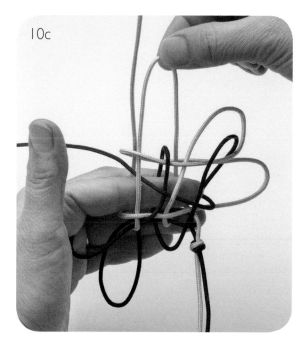

11a

10d

11b

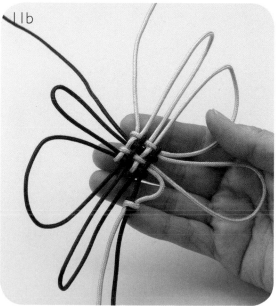

Tightening and adjusting

To shorten your strands and adjust the length of the loops around the centre motif, locate the direction of the weave on both sides for each strand, beginning at the starting knot and going towards the end. Follow the direction of the weave as indicated by the numbered arrows on the photograph of the knot, shown just before final tightening and adjusting. Always adjust one side of your work and then the other (left/right).

Direction of the weave: back.

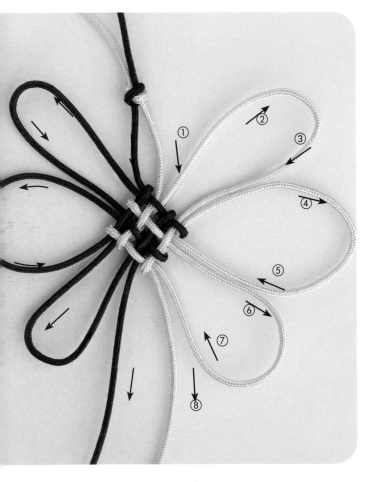

Direction of the weave: front.

Final steps

Turn your work over lengthways so the starting knot is at the top. Lay your work out right side up. Start by tightening one of the two strands that separate the chrysanthemum from the starting knot. To do this, insert your awl into the bottom of the first row of weaving (12a) and pull the strand gently (12b) to create a loop. Follow the extension of the strand in your work and pull (12c). Continue to locate the extension of the strand across your centre motif (12d), adjusting the loops one by one and always following the direction of the weave.

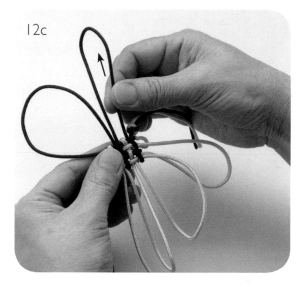

12c

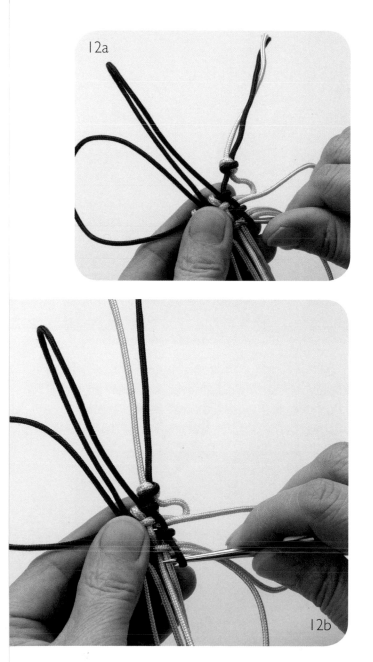

12a

12b

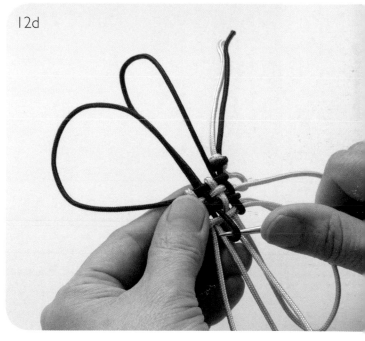

12d

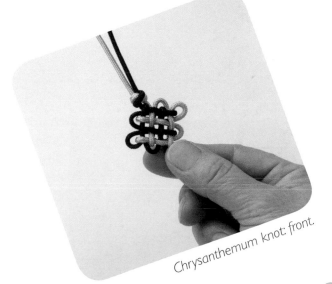

Chrysanthemum knot: front.

7 Take the loose end and pass it under the two strands of the first loop from back to front, leaving about 10cm (4in) behind it (7a). Next, bend the strand back on itself to form a fourth loop, identical to the three other loops. Hold this loop halfway up, between your right thumb and index finger (7b).

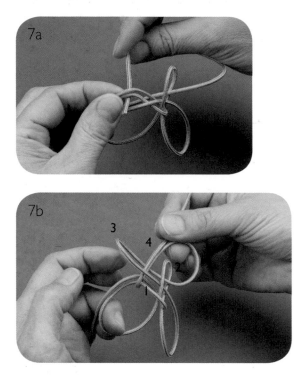
7a

7b
3
4
2
1

8 Pull the two strands of the fourth loop, on the right, and the two strands of the first loop, on the left. Place your middle fingers inside the two large loops that appear on each side. Place your ring fingers and little fingers inside the large loop that appears between the previous two loops. Lastly, pull all the strands at the same time to tighten the loops and the ginger knot.

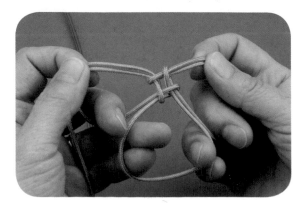

Turn your left hand 90 degrees to the left. Your three loops should now be on the right and the loose end on the left.

9 To shorten your three large loops, follow the direction of the weave from the starting point of your tightening and adjusting to the end of the strand. The centre motif of the ginger knot is made up of four interwoven strands in the shape of a diamond. Using your awl, pull the strand in the top right of the diamond to create a loop. The strand that forms the loop at the bottom of the diamond will get shorter (9a and 9b). Tighten the centre motif by pulling on the extension of the strand on the reverse of the knot (9c). Shorten the two remaining loops in this way, always following the direction of the weave (9d). Each time you move a strand, hold all the other strands in the centre motif secure.

9a

9b

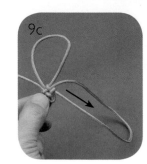
9c

9d

10 Turn your work over so the left strand (dark green) is on the right. Taking your starting point at 30cm (12in) from the starting knot, follow the instructions from step 2 to step 9 to make up a second ginger knot. When you have finished, turn your work over again so your strands are in their original position (dark green on the left and pale green on the right).

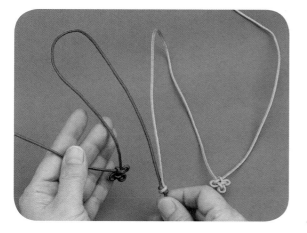

11 Place your starting knot at the base of your right palm. Pass the right strand (pale green) behind your hand. Place the left strand (dark green) on your hand and wind it around twice. Place your left index finger into the bottom of the two vertical loops you have made around your right hand (loop 1 on the right and loop 2 on the left). Next, as you remove your right hand, secure the base of the loops between your left index finger and middle finger (see page 63, chrysanthemum knot, steps 1 and 2). Place your left ginger knot at the base of loop 2 and take the end of the strand over to the left, between your thumb and index finger.

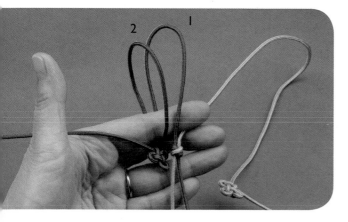

12 Hold the back strand (pale green) between your left index and middle fingers, and bring it round to the right of your left hand. Make a third loop: bring the end of the strand round to the starting point of the loop, leaving about 8cm (3in) between this point and the ginger knot. Secure the strand once more between your left index and middle fingers, passing it over the top of the first strand in the loop. Leave the end extending from loop 3 to hang towards the back of your work.

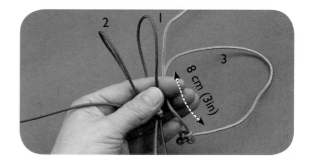

13 Take the back strand of loop 3 and bring it to the front of loops 1 and 2 and in front of your left index finger. Place it horizontally around the two vertical loops, then bring it to the front between your index finger and middle finger (13a). Take the front strand of loop 3 and cross it over the back strand. Hold the cross you have made between your left index finger and middle finger. You have now created two new loops from loop 3: loop 4, which surrounds loops 1 and 2, and loop 5, after the last cross you made (13b).

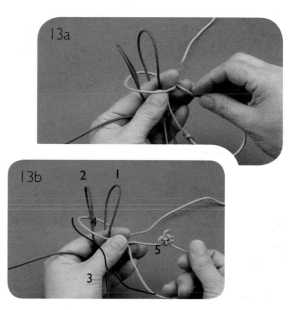

14 Take the left strand (dark green) that extends from loops 1 and 2 and thread it into loops 1 and 2 from left to right (14a). Pass it underneath the other end (14b), then into loop 5 from back to front (14c). Secure it at the base of this loop between your left index finger and middle finger. Next, bring the strand over to the left and thread it through loops 1 and 2 from right to left. Pull the strand gently, passing it in front of your left index finger (14d). Secure with your thumb.

15 Take the back strand of loop 5 and bring it to the front to undo the cross at the base of the loop (15a). Take the strand that is now at the back of the loop and repeat step 13. You now have two new loops: loop 6, the second loop surrounding loops 1 and 2, and loop 7, after the last cross you made (15b, 15c and 15d).

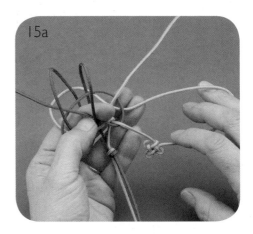

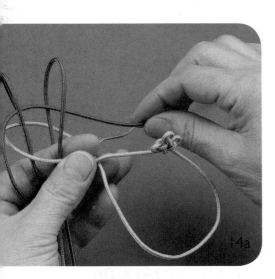

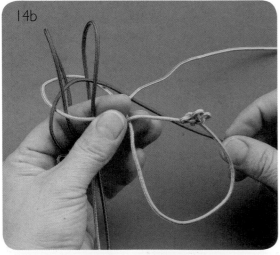

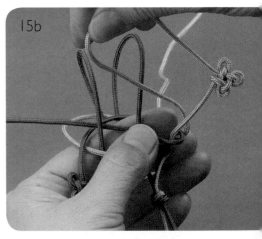

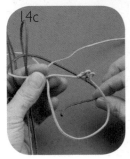

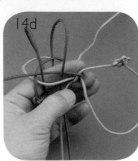

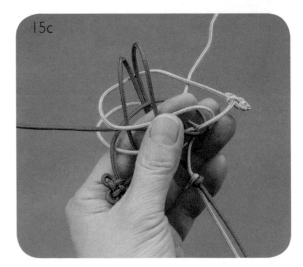

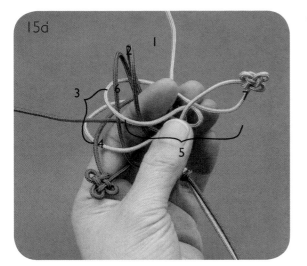

15d

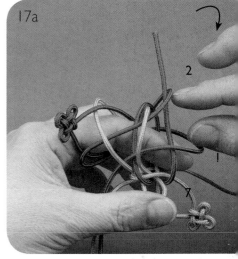

17a

17 Turn your left hand 90 degrees so loop 7 is now at the bottom of your work and loops 1 and 2 are on the horizontal. Spread them out (17a). Take the end from the back (pale green) and weave horizontally from right to left, passing behind, in front, behind and in front of the four vertical strands located between loops 1 and 2 (17b). Next, thread the end through the bottom of loop 2 (17c).

16 Pick up the left strand again (dark green) and repeat step 14: thread it into loops 1 and 2 from left to right. Thread it behind the other end (16a), then into loop 7 from back to front. Secure it at the base of this loop between your left index finger and middle finger. Next, bring the end round to the left and thread it through loops 1 and 2 from right to left. Pull the strand gently, passing it in front of your left index finger (16b).

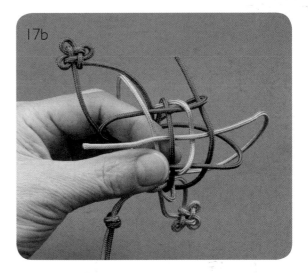

17b

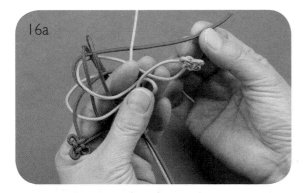

16a

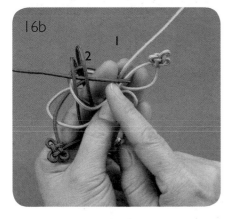

16b

17c

Butterfly Knot

There are several different versions of this knot. The design shown here is known as the female butterfly knot. The wings are made up first, followed by a chrysanthemum motif for the body. The butterfly is a symbol of longevity and conjugal bliss, and also represents joy and summer.

1 Work with two 1m (39¼in) lengths of cord tied together at one end, or with one 2m (78½in) length of cord. If using a single length of cord, mark the middle by tying a short length of fine thread in the centre, then tie a basic knot (see page 11). Start by working with the right strand (1a). Hold your starting point firmly between your left index finger and thumb, 12cm (4¾in) from the starting knot (1b).

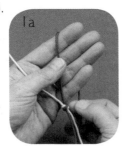

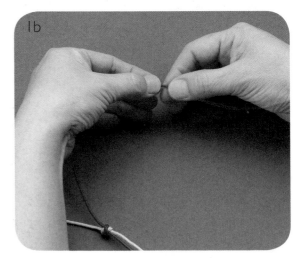

2 Pick up the strand 12cm (4³/₄in) from your starting point. Make your first loop by crossing the end of the strand over your starting point. As you form the loop, ensure that the end of the strand goes over to the right. Secure this first loop between your left index finger and thumb.

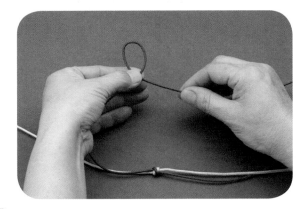

3 Take the end of the right strand approximately 12cm (4³/₄in) from the first loop and make a second loop in exactly the same way as the first (see step 2 above). Place the second loop on top of the first and hold it at its base between your left thumb and index finger (3a). Place the strand extending from the second loop to the left of the strand at the base of the first loop and then thread it underneath and out to the right (3b).

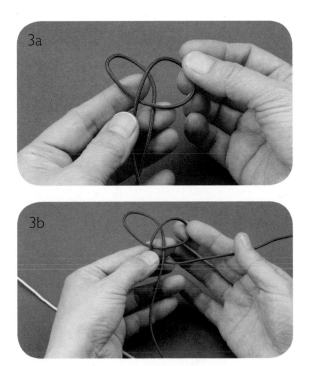

3a

3b

4 Keep working with the same strand. Thread it into the two loops from right to left, going over the right strand of the second loop, under the right strand of the first loop, over the left strand of the second loop and lastly under the left strand of the first loop (4a). Gently pull the end of the strand to the left: a third loop will appear to the right of the first two loops (4b). Tighten the third and first loops to make a wing knot, leaving the middle loop untightened: pull on the far end of the strand and on the strand at the base of the first loop (4c). Pull the top of the middle loop outwards to keep its original size.

4a

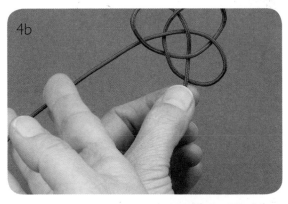

4b

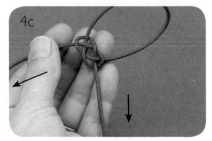

4c

5 Turn your work over so the left strand is now on the right, and make up a second wing knot using the left strand by following the instructions in steps 1 to 4. To make the two butterfly wings completely symmetrical, reverse the over-under pattern in the strands from your first wing. Now turn your work over again so the strands are in their original position.

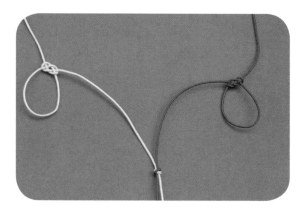

7 Place your left index finger into the bottom of the two vertical loops you made around your right hand (loop 1 on the right, loop 2 above the wing knot on the left) (7a). Next, as you remove your right hand, hold the loops at their base between your left thumb and index finger (7b).

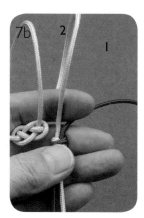

6 Place the starting knot in the base of your right palm. Pass the right strand (dark pink) behind your hand. Place the left strand (mauve) in your hand, then place your hand inside the loop at the top of the wing knot (6a). Lastly, bring the end of the strand to the front of your hand, on the left-hand side, and secure it between your right index finger and thumb (6b).

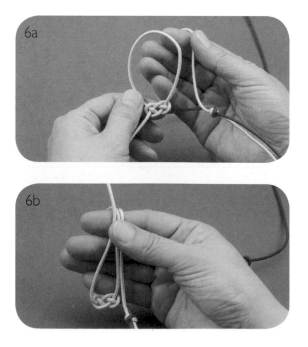

8 Hold the back strand (dark pink) between your left index finger and middle finger, and bring it out to the right of your left hand (8a). Make a third loop: bring the end of the strand back to the starting point of the loop, leaving 8cm (3in) between the wing knot and the starting point. Again, secure the strand between your left index finger and middle finger, passing it on top of the first strand in the loop (8b). Leave the end extending from loop 3 to hang to the back of your work.

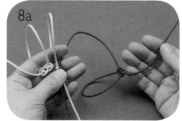

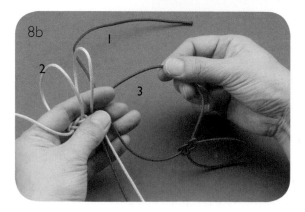

9 Take the back strand of loop 3 and bring it in front of loops 1 and 2 and in front of your left index finger. Loop it horizontally over the two vertical loops, then bring the strand to the front between your index finger and middle finger (9a and 9b). Now take the front strand of loop 3 and cross it over the back strand (9c).

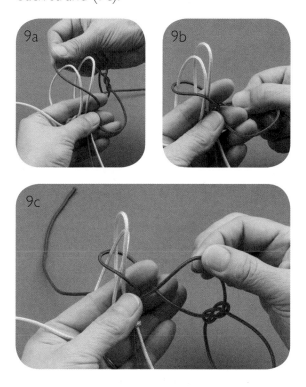

Secure the cross you have just made between your left index finger and middle finger. You have now made two new loops from loop 3: loop 4, which surrounds loops 1 and 2, and loop 5, after the last cross you made (9d).

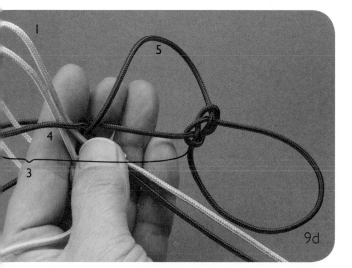

10 Take the left strand (mauve) that extends from loops 1 and 2 and thread it into these two loops from left to right (10a). Thread it behind the other end (10b), then into loop 5 from back to front (10c).

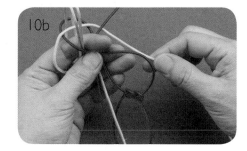

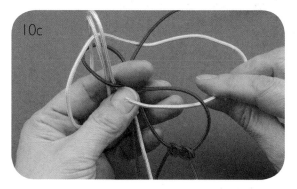

Secure the end at the base of this loop between your left index finger and middle finger. Next, bring the strand over to the left and thread it through loops 1 and 2 from right to left, passing it in front of your left index finger. Pull the end gently (10d).

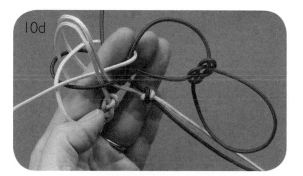

11 Take the back strand of loop 5 and bring it to the front to undo the cross at the base of the loop (11a). Next, take the back strand of loop 6 at the top of the wing knot (11b). Pass it in front of loops 1 and 2, so that these two loops go through loop 6 (11c). Hold the back strand of loop 6 between your left index finger and middle finger (11d).

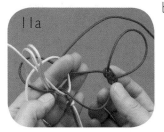

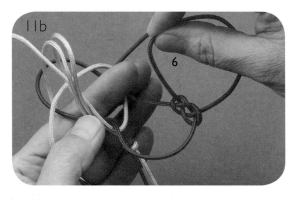

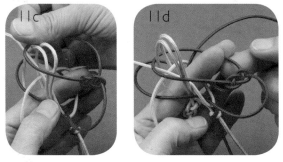

Pick up the front strand of loop 5 again, at the base of the wing knot, and cross it over the front strand of loop 6. You now have a new loop, loop 7, located after the last cross you made (11e). Secure it with your left thumb.

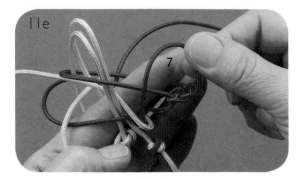

12 Pick up the left end again (mauve) and repeat step 10. Thread it into loops 1 and 2 from left to right (12a). Pass it behind the other end (dark pink) (12b) and into loop 7 from back to front (12c). Pull the end of the strand to the left and thread it through loops 1 and 2 from right to left (12d).

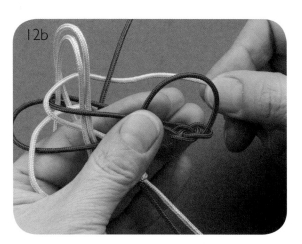

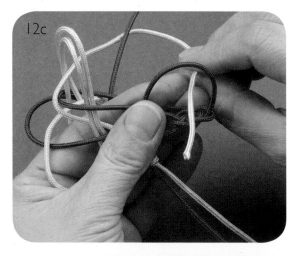

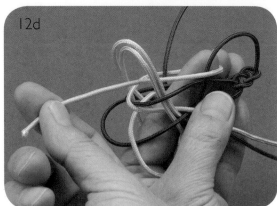

13 Turn your left hand 90 degrees so loop 7 is now at the bottom of your work and loops 1 and 2 are on the horizontal (13a).

14 Placing your index finger between loops 1 and 2, turn your work over so the working end is on the right (dark pink) (14a). Thread the end into the base of loop 1 from back to front (14b). Weave horizontally from right to left, passing in front, behind, in front and lastly behind the four vertical strands located between loops 1 and 2 (14c and 14d). Pull gently on the end.

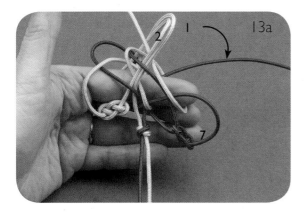

Spread the loops out (13b). Take the end from the back (dark pink) (13c) and weave horizontally from right to left, passing behind, in front, behind and in front of the four vertical strands located between loops 1 and 2 (13d). Take your left hand out of the knot (13e).

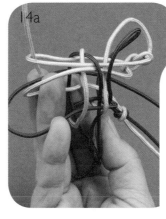

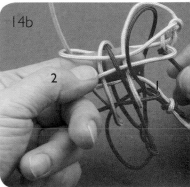

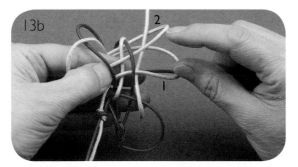

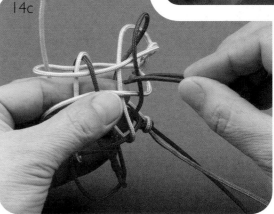

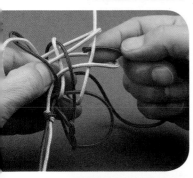

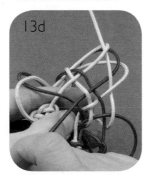

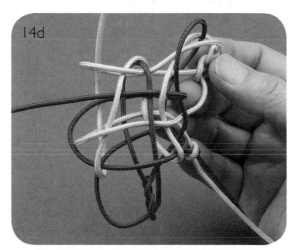

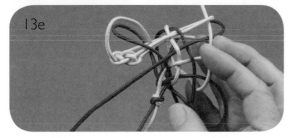

15 Pull the wing knot on the right (mauve) outwards (15a). Next, pull the loop located just above (mauve) (15b). Turn your work over lengthways and widthways (15c). Pull the second wing knot outwards (15d), then pull the loop just below it downwards (15e).

15d

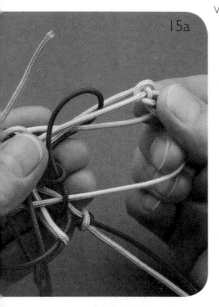

15a

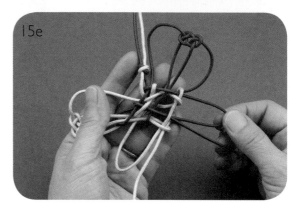

15e

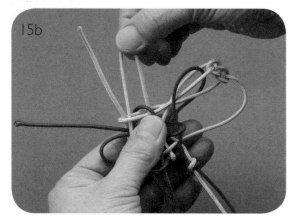

15b

16 To tighten the butterfly's body, continue to pull the two wing knots and the two loops mentioned in step 15 (16a). Now pull evenly on all the strands around your work (16b).

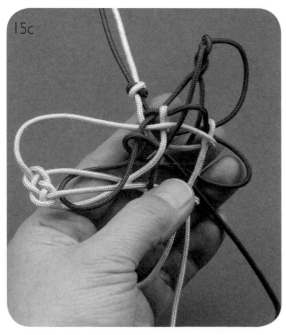

15c

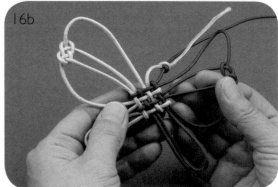

16a

16b

Finishing & shaping

Tightening and adjusting

To shorten the strands around the body of the butterfly and adjust the length of the wings, locate the direction of the weave on both sides for each strand, from the starting knot to the end of the cord (17a). To follow the direction of the weave in the butterfly's body, work in exactly the same way as for the chrysanthemum knot (see step 12, page 70). Shape one side of your work, then the other, working first with one strand and then a second.

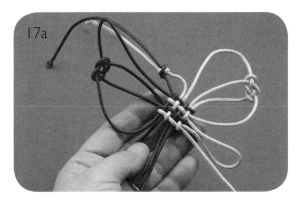

Final steps

Start by shortening one of the two strands between the body of the butterfly and the starting knot. To do this, insert your awl into the bottom of the first row of weaving (17b) and pull the strand gently to form a loop. Follow the extension of the strand in your weaving and pull (17c). Continue locating the extension of the strand through the wing knot and through the butterfly's body, always following the direction of the weave.

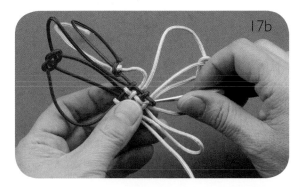

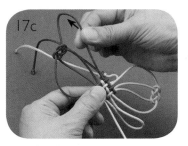

Adjustments

To neaten out your work, adjust the lengths of the strands as follows (17d).

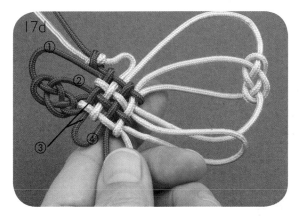

① Leave 4cm (1½in) between the top of the body and the top of the wing knot.

② Shorten the strand located just beneath, between the wing knot and the upper edge of the body, to 2cm (¾in).

③ Bring the two strands at the base of the wing knot up close to the body.

④ Make a small loop below the wing knot at the bottom of the body.

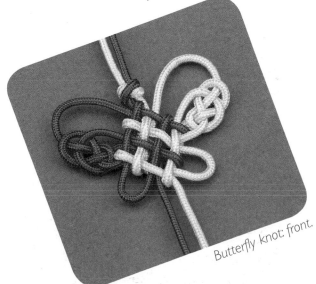

Butterfly knot: front.

Jewellery and accessories

Simple necklace

Materials required

To make one 60cm (23¹/₂in) necklace:
- 1m (39¹/₄in) fine cord in mauve
- 1 semi-precious stone pendant 5cm (2in) in diameter

Featured knot

Ring (four-unit ball), see page 22.

Threading on your pendant

Halve your cord and thread the loop through the hole in your pendant from back to front. Take the two strands at the other end of the cord and thread them through this loop. Pull both strands at the same time to tighten, ensuring that they remain the same length.

Sliding clasp: first half

Lay the two ends out vertically in front of you with the pendant right side up. Place the right strand over your left index finger and leave the end out to the left. Take the left strand 20cm (8in) from the pendant and tie a four-unit ball ring knot around the right strand and your left index finger. Once you have tightened the knot, move it to the end of the left strand.

Sliding clasp: second half

Turn your work over so your pendant is on the reverse. Pull the loose end through the ring knot until you have a length of approximately 30cm (12in) and make up a second ring knot to the right of the first, around the other strand. Once you have tightened the knot, move it to the end of the strand.

Finishing off

Move the two ring knots along the strands so they lie equidistant from the pendant. Ensure that the knots slide easily along the strands and trim any excess cord close to each knot.

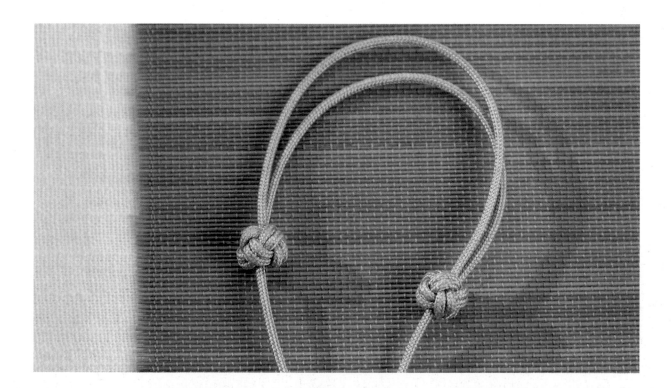

Smart cufflinks

Materials required
To make one pair of knot cufflinks:
* *1m (39¼in) fine cord in the colour of your choice*

Featured knot
Ring (four-unit or five-unit ball), see page 22.

These cufflinks are made from fine cord and are shown here in a smaller version (four-unit ring knot) about 8mm (⁵/₁₆in) in diameter and a larger version (five-unit ring knot) approximately 1cm (³/₈in) in diameter. Choose the model that fits your buttonhole.

First ring knot

Make up a four-unit or five-unit ring knot, starting from the middle of your cord. Tighten it and move it to the right end of your cord.

Second ring knot

Turn your work over so the first knot is now on the left. Take the right strand and make up a ring knot identical to the first one. Move it along the strand towards the first knot, leaving 1cm (³/₈in) between the two knots.

Doubling up the centre

Insert your hook into your second ring knot (on the right-hand side) from left to right. Pick up the loose end on the far side of the second knot in the end of the hook and pull the hook back through the knot. Gently pull the loose end. Insert the hook into the first ring knot (on the left-hand side) from left to right. Again, pick up the loose end with the end of the hook and pull the hook back through the knot. Gently pull the strand to adjust its length between the two knots.

Finishing off

Locate the end of the strand that doubles the weave of the first ring knot (on the left). Use your awl to take out its last two movements through the knot. Replace these with the loose end, using your hook to help thread the strand into the weave of the ball. Trim the end close to the knot. If needed, hide the ends in the knot using your awl.

Make up the second cufflink in the same way with the remaining cord. Adjust its length and tightening to match the first cufflink so the pair are identical.

Beautiful beads

Bead necklace

Featured knots
Double connection, see page 14.
Ring (four-unit ball), see page 22.

Beads
Cut four 1m (39¹/₄in) lengths of cord. Make up five four-unit ring knots from each of these lengths (20 in total). Tighten them into a ball and trim any excess cord.

Clasp: loop
Locate the middle of the remaining cord and halve it. Leave a 1.5cm (⁵/₈in) loop at the start, then tie a double connection knot.

Threading on the beads
Leave a 6.5cm (2¹/₂in) gap after the first double connection knot and tie a second knot. Thread two flat beads on to the two strands at the same time. Next, using your hook (see page 10), thread on a ring knot. Continue in this way, alternating between one flat bead and one ring knot. Once you have added knot 20, thread on two flat beads. Tie a double connection knot to secure your beads. Leave a 6.5cm (2¹/₂in) gap and tie a final double connection knot.

Clasp: ball
Tie a ring knot as follows. Place the last double connection knot at the base of your left index finger and follow the instructions for the four-unit ring knot from step 2 to step 6 (see page 23), working with both strands at once. Ensure that the two strands remain parallel at all times.

At the end of step 6, move straight to the tightening and adjusting stage, following the instructions in step 8 (ball version). Use your hook (see page 10) to thread the loose ends into the knot. Trim the excess.

Adjustable bracelet

Featured knot
Ring (four-unit ball), see page 22.

First ring knot
Starting in the centre of your cord, take the right end and make up a four-unit ball ring knot. Tighten and move to the end of the right strand.

Threading on the beads and adjusting the size
Thread your two beads on to the left strand. Insert your hook into the ring knot from left to right. Pick up the loose end on the left of the knot in the end of your hook and pull the hook back through the knot. Gently pull the strand and thread it through the two beads from right to left, ensuring it does not twist. Leave 40cm (15³/₄in) at the end to make a second knot.

Second ring knot
Turn your work over so the left loose end is now on the right and tie a ring knot to match the first around the strand that forms your bracelet. Adjust the bracelet to fit your wrist by moving the second ring knot towards the end of the strand. Ensure that the knots slide easily along the strands and trim the excess close to each knot.

Back to nature

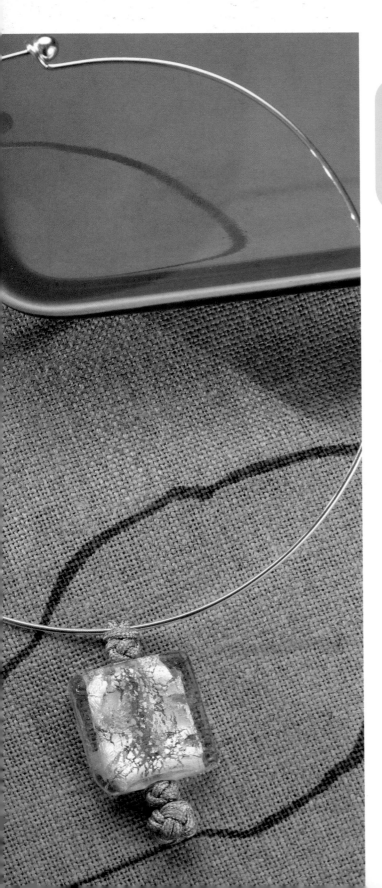

Choker

Materials required
• 80cm (31¹/₂in) fine cord in pale green
• 1 square glass bead with 2.5cm (1in)
sides, with hole at least 4mm (³/₁₆in)
in diameter)
• 1 silver choker

Featured knots
*Double connection, see
page 14.
Lotus, see page 18.
Ring (five-unit ball),
see page 22.*

Attaching the cord to your choker
Halve the cord and position the loop so it
sits across the choker from front to back.
Thread the ends of the cord through this
loop. Pull both strands at the same time to
tighten, ensuring that they remain exactly the
same length.

Pendant
Position the two strands so they hang
downwards and tie a lotus knot. Tighten and
bring it to the base of the strands so it sits
next to the choker. Thread the bead on to
both strands at the same time. Make up another lotus knot. Tighten the knot and slide it
up so it sits against the bead.

Now tie a five-unit ball ring knot: place the
lotus at the base of your left index finger
and follow the instructions for the ring knot,
working with both strands at the same time.
Keep the two stands parallel at all times. At
the end of step 6, go directly to the tightening
and adjusting stage, following the instructions
in step 8 (ball version). Using your hook (see
page 10), thread the loose ends into the knot,
then trim the excess. If needed, hide them in
the knot using your awl.

Necklace

Materials required
To make one 40cm (15³/₄in) necklace:
• *4.5m (177in) fine cord in dark green*
• *1 large glass or resin novelty
bead 4cm (1¹/₂in) long in green
(with hole at least 8mm (⁵/₁₆in) in
diameter)*

Featured knots
*Double connection,
see page 14.
Lotus, see page 18.
Ring (five-unit ball),
see page 22.*

Clasp: loop

Locate the centre of the cord and halve it.
Leave an approximately 1.5cm (⁵/₈in) loop
at the start of your necklace, then tie a double connection knot.

Necklace knots

Position the loose ends so they hang
downwards. Tie a lotus knot, using the double connection knot at the base of the loop
as your starting knot. Next, tie 37 double
connection knots, two lotus knots, five double connection knots, two lotus knots, 37
double connection knots, one lotus knot
and one last double connection knot. As you
work, tighten each knot against the previous
knot. Thread your bead into the centre of
the necklace so it sits between two pairs of
lotus knots.

Clasp: ball

Make up a ring knot as follows. Place the last
double connection knot at the base of your
left index finger and follow the instructions
for the five-unit ring knot (see page 28), working with the two strands at the same time.
Always keep the two strands parallel. At the
end of step 6, go directly to the tightening
and adjusting stage, following the instructions
in step 8 (ball version). Using your hook (see
page 10), thread the loose ends into the knot
and trim the excess. If needed, hide the ends
in the knot using your awl.

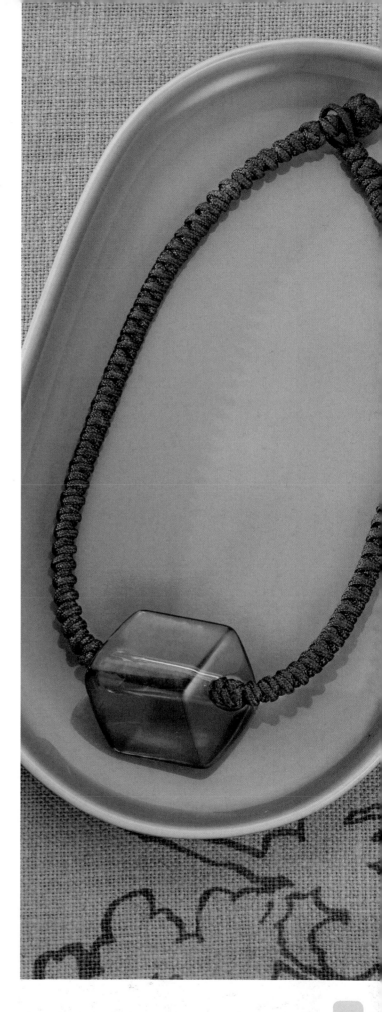

Autumn brooch

Materials required

To make one brooch:
- 2 x 2m (78½in) fine cord in the colours of your choice
- 1 gold hat pin

Featured knot
Ring knot, see page 22.

Small ring

To make a flat seven-unit ring knot, follow the instructions for the four-unit ring knot. When you get to step 2, wind the cord twice around your left hand (rather than your left index finger). After step 5, repeat steps 3, 4 and 5 once and steps 3 and 4 once. Skip directly to step 7 to double up your weaving. Now repeat the process a further two times to triple and quadruple your work. Next, tighten and finish off your work, following the instructions in step 8 (flat version).

Large ring

To make a flat eight-unit ring knot, follow the instructions for the five-unit ring knot. When you get to step 2, wind the cord twice around your left hand (rather than your left index finger). After step 5, repeat steps 3, 4 and 5 once and steps 3 and 4 once. Skip directly to step 7 to double up your weaving. Now repeat the process a further two times to triple and quadruple your work. Next, tighten and finish off your work, following the instructions in step 8 (flat version).

Place the two rings one on top of the other and push them on to a hat pin.

Variant

Why not sew these knots on to a bag or an item of clothing?

Trendy belt

Materials required

To make one adjustable belt approx. 1.2m (47in) long:
- *1.5m (59in) thick cord in black*
- *1.5m (59in) thick cord in plum*
- *1m (39¼in) fine cord in maroon*
- *1m (39¼in) fine cord in purple*
- *1m (39¼in) fine cord in plum*
- *50cm (20in) fine cord in black*

Featured knot

*Ring (four-unit ball),
see page 22.*

The beads

Make up seven four-unit ball ring knots from your fine cord in the following colours: two maroon, two purple, two plum, one black. Tighten them and trim the excess to make your beads.

Threading on your beads

Use your hook (see page 10) to thread your seven beads one by one on to your two thick black and plum cords at the same time, in the following order: one plum, one purple, one maroon, one black, one maroon, one purple, one plum. Thread them into the centre of your thick cords.

Belt adjuster: first half

Lay out the two loose ends on each side vertically in front of you. Place the two right strands over your left index finger, guiding the ends out to the left. Pick up the two left strands approximately 50cm (20in) from their ends. Tie a four-unit ring knot around the right strands and your left index finger with the two strands at the same time (see page 23, steps 2 to 6). Ensure the two strands remain parallel and avoid twisting the cords. At the end of step 6, skip straight to the tightening and adjusting stage, following the instructions in step 8 (see page 26, ball version). Once you have tightened the knot,

move it to the end of the two left strands (to move the ring knot along the strands, work with the two strands in your weaving at the same time). Using your hook (see page 10), thread the loose ends into the knot, then trim the excess. If needed, hide them in the knot using your awl.

Belt adjuster: second half

Turn your work over from right to left. Pull the two loose ends through the ring knot to a length of approximately 50cm (20in) and tie a second ring knot to the right of the first – again using the two strands together – around the two other strands. Work in exactly the same way as for the first half of the belt adjuster and avoid twisting your threads. Ensure that the belt adjuster slides easily and adjust to fit.

Summer jewellery

Choker

Materials required
- *50cm (20in) fine cord in pink*
- *50cm (20in) fine cord in violet*
- *50cm (20in) fine cord in lime green*
- *50cm (20in) fine cord in mustard yellow*
- *1 silver choker*

Featured knot
Spectacle, see page 30.

Cord assembly

Take one length of cord at its centre and position it so that it sits either side of the choker. Keep the back strand on the right and the front strand on the left. Secure the two strands with a short length of fine thread while you tie your knot.

The knot

Make up a spectacle knot. Move the knot along the strands so that only a small loop remains around the choker. Ensure that the strands remain in their starting position around the choker. Remove the thread from around the strands at the base of the knot.

Fringe

Take one of the two strands at the end of the knot. Pull on the core inside the strand. Trim the core close to the knot and gently unravel the threads on the outside of your strand. Repeat with the other strand. To obtain a smooth and even fringe, iron the threads and trim them carefully 1cm (3/8in) below the knot.

Repeat this process three times to make up the four knots on your choker.

Earrings

Materials required
- *2 x 50cm (20in) fine cord in pink*
- *2 earring fishhooks*

Featured knot
Spectacle, see page 30.

Take one length of cord at its centre and thread it through the loop in your earring finding. Tie a spectacle knot with a 5cm (2in) fringe, using exactly the same process as for the knots on the choker. Repeat for the second earring. Adjust the tightening of your knots and the length of the fringes to ensure the pair are identical.

By the sea

Materials required
To make one 40cm (15³/₄in) necklace:
- *2.7m (106¹/₄in) fine cord in sea green*
- *1 shell disc*

Featured knots
Double connection, see page 14.
Ring (four-unit ball), see page 22.
Spectacle, see page 30.

Clasp: loop

Cut a 2m (78¹/₂in) length of cord and halve it. Leave a 1.5cm (⁵/₈in) loop at the start of your necklace, then tie a double connection knot.

Centre motif

Leave a 14.5cm (5³/₄in) gap after the first double connection knot and tie another. Next, tie seven spectacle knots in succession, keeping them as close together as possible. Tie one double connection knot. Leave a 14.5cm (5³/₄in) gap and tie a final double connection knot.

Clasp: ball

Follow the instructions for the ball of the clasp on the bead necklace (page 94).

The pendant

Insert your hook just above the middle strand at the base of the fourth spectacle knot, from back to front. Take your remaining 70cm (27¹/₂in) length of cord, halve it, thread it into the end of your hook and pull it to the back of the knot. Adjust the length of each strand of cord so that the right strand measures approximately 20cm (8in) and the left strand 50cm (20in). Thread the two ends of cord into the small loop behind the knot. Pull both strands together to tighten. Take the left strand and tie a four-unit ball ring knot around the right strand. Tighten it against the spectacle knot. Thread the right strand through the hole in the pendant.

Finishing off

Locate the end of the strand that doubles the weave of your ring knot. Using your awl, take out its last two movements through the knot. Replace them with the loose end on the right, using your hook to help thread the strand into the ball. Bring the pendant to the bottom of the ring knot, then trim the excess. If needed, hide the ends in the knot using your awl.

Dragonflies

Materials required

For each dragonfly::
- 1m (39¼in) fine cord in the colour of your choice

To make one brooch:
- 1 brooch mount
- needle and thread

To make one keyring:
- 1 keyring
- 2 jump rings 8mm (⁵/₁₆in) in diameter
- 5cm (2in) chain
- flat-nosed pliers

To make one bag charm:
- 1 trigger clasp
- 5 jump rings 8mm (⁵/₁₆in) in diameter
- 2 jump rings 5mm (¼in) in diameter
- flat-nosed pliers

Featured knot
Dragonfly, see page 36.

Dragonfly keyring.

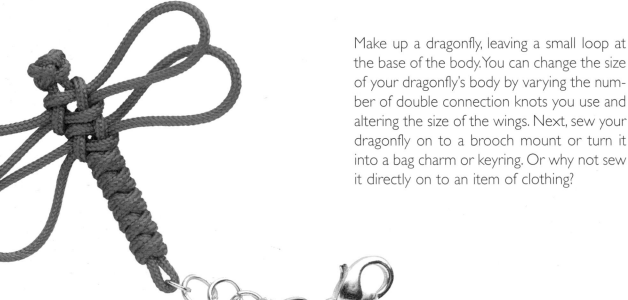

Dragonfly bag charm.

Make up a dragonfly, leaving a small loop at the base of the body. You can change the size of your dragonfly's body by varying the number of double connection knots you use and altering the size of the wings. Next, sew your dragonfly on to a brooch mount or turn it into a bag charm or keyring. Or why not sew it directly on to an item of clothing?

Moonlight

Materials required
To make an approx. 80cm (31¹/₁₂in) necklace:
• 2.5m (98¹/₂in) satin cord 2.5mm (¹/₁₀in) in diameter in dark pink
• 1 semi-precious stone disc 4.5cm (1³/₄in) in diameter

Featured knots
Double connection, see page 14.
Ring (four-unit ball), see page 22.
Ginger, see page 42.

Attaching the stone

Thread your stone into the centre of your satin cord and tie a double connection knot. Tie three ginger knots in succession, increasing the size of the small side loops with each knot.

Working the ends

Take one of the strands from the top of your last ginger knot and measure a 50cm (20in) length. Mark this point by tying a short length of fine thread around it. Lay the end of the strand on the left and tie a ginger knot. When you tighten the knot, shorten the length on the left of the knot on the left strand and the length on the right of the knot on the right strand, so that approximately 50cm (20in) remains between the centre motif of the necklace and the ginger knot at the end of the strand. With the free end, tie a four-unit ball-shaped ring knot around the other strand on top of the ginger knot. Tighten the ring knot against the ginger knot and trim the excess close to the ring knot. Repeat this process with the other end of the necklace.

Rising sun

Materials required

To make one pair of earrings:
- *2 x 80cm (31 ¹/₂in) fine cord in red*
- *2 gold earring fishhooks*
- *2 glass drop beads with rings*

Featured knots
*Double connection,
see page 14.
Ring (four-unit ball),
see page 22.
Ginger, see page 42.*

Bead assembly and knotwork

Thread your bead into the centre of one length of cord. Tie five ginger knots in succession, increasing the size of the small side loops with each knot.

When tying several ginger knots in succession, always turn your last ginger knot on to the reverse before starting the next. This will ensure that all the knots are facing the right way when you turn your finished piece over.

Finishing off

Thread one of the two strands at the top of your last ginger knot into the ring of your earring finding. Tie a four-unit ball ring knot with this strand, beginning approximately 3mm (¹/₈in) from the ring. Locate the end of the strand that doubles up the weave of the ring knot. Using your awl, take out its last two movements through the knot. Replace them with the other loose end at the top of the last ginger knot, using your hook to pass the strand into the weave of the ball. Trim the excess. If needed, hide the ends in the weave with your awl.

Repeat this process to make up another earring. Adjust the tightening of your knots and the length to match the first so the pair are identical.

Lucky charm

Materials required
- 4m (157in) fine cord in green
- 1m (39¼in) fine cord in red
- silk or cotton embroidery thread

Featured knots
Double connection, see page 14.
Lotus, see page 18.
Ring (four-unit ball), see page 22.
Dragonfly wings, see dragonfly knot, page 37, steps 2 to 5.
Strawberry, see page 48.

Top loop

Locate the centre of the green cord and halve it. Leave a 5cm (2in) loop at the start of your lucky charm, then tie a double connection knot. At the top of the double connection knot, wind a length of fine red thread around the strands over approximately 5mm (¼in) to decorate the base of the loop. Hide the knot.

Knots

Take your red cord and tie three four-unit ring knots in it. Tighten them into a ball and trim the strands close to the knots. Pick up your green cord again and place the loop at the bottom of your work and the loose ends at the top. Use the double connection knot as your starting knot. Tie one strawberry knot (follow the instructions for the strawberry knot from step 2, page 48) and one double connection knot, and tighten them against each other. Repeat this series of knots twice.

Fringes

Hold the last double connection knot and the loose ends at the top of your work. Make a pair of dragonfly wings (see page 37, steps 2 to 5), adjusting the length of the loops so they measure 16.5cm (6½in) on each side. Make a second pair of wings, adjusting the length of the loops to 15cm (6in) this time. Turn your work over so the ends are hanging downwards. Tie two lotus knots, using the previous knots as a starting knot. Turn your work over again so the ends are now at the top. Make up two dragonfly wings in the same way as the previous two pairs of wings, adjusting the length of the loops to 14cm (5½in) this time. Tie a double connection knot.

Finishing off

Take one of the ends and tie a four-unit ball ring knot around the other strand. Move the ring knot along so it sits snugly beside the last double connection knot. Locate the end of the strand that doubles the weave of your ring knot. Using your awl, remove its last two movements through the knot. Replace them with the other loose end, making a loop 12cm (4¾in) in length after your ring knot. Use your hook to thread the strand into the weave of your ring knot. Tighten and trim the excess cord. If needed, hide the ends inside the knot using your awl.

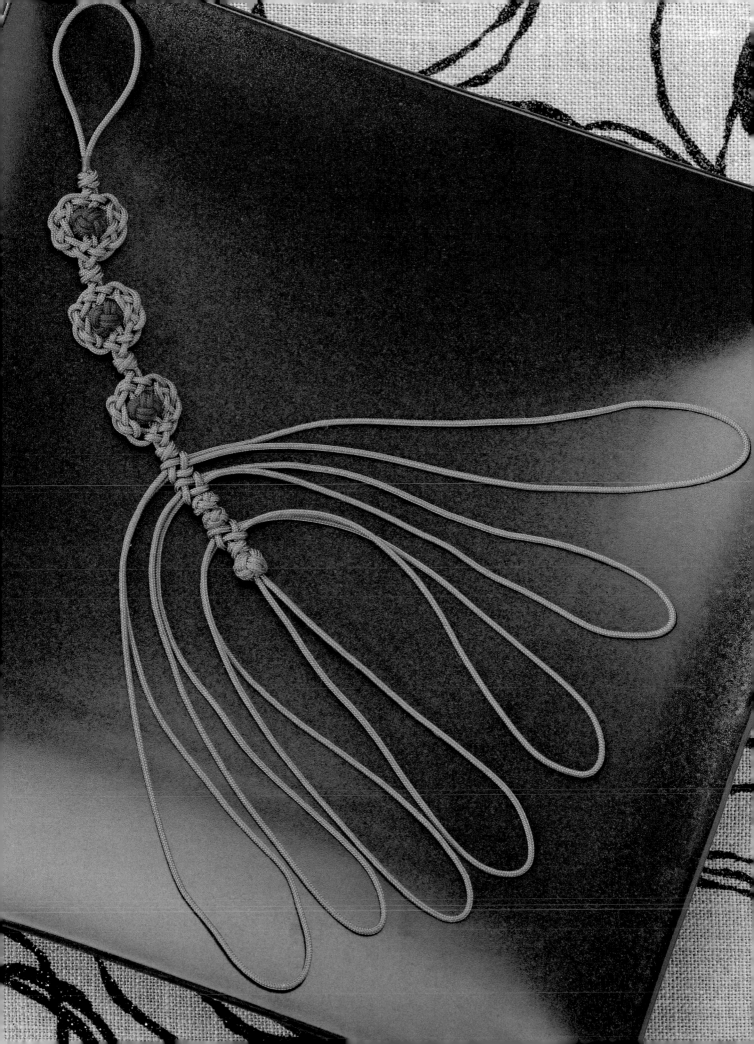

Plum blossom

Materials required

To make one chain necklace approx. 1.5m (59in) long:
- *2 x 2m (78¹/₂in) fine cord in purple*
- *3 flat glass beads 1.5cm (⁵/₈in) in diameter (with a hole at least 3mm (¹/₈in) in diameter)*

Featured knots

Ring (four-unit ball), see page 22.
Plum blossom, see page 56.

Threading on the beads

Tie a four-unit ball ring knot at the end of one of your lengths of cord. Thread one bead on to the longest end and trim the far end at the base of the knot. Follow the instructions for the four-unit ring knot from step 2 to step 6, without doubling the weave of the knot. After step 6, skip straight to the tightening and adjusting stage to form a basic ring knot. Thread on a bead and tie another basic ring knot as before. Then thread on another bead.

Centre motif

Make up a four-unit ball ring knot at one of the ends of the second length of cord, then trim the excess at the base of the knot. Pick up your first cord. Using your hook (see page 10), thread the loose end extending from the last bead into the ring knot. Tighten the knot against the bead. You should now have two ends at the top of your ring knot. Lay your work out vertically in front of you and tie a plum blossom knot, using the ring knot as your starting knot.

Make four small matching loops all the way around your plum blossom knot and move it along so it sits against the ring knot. Tie a double connection knot and then tie a second plum blossom knot, using the double connection knot as a starting knot. Make two small loops at the bottom of the plum blossom knot and two slightly larger loops at the top. Ensure that these last two knots sit tightly against each other.

Necklace ends

Take one of the strands at the top of the last plum blossom knot and measure a 70cm (27¹/₂in) length. Mark this point by tying a short length of fine thread around it. Place the end of the strand on the left and tie a plum blossom knot. When you tighten the knot, shorten the lengths on the left of the knot on the left strand and the lengths on the right of the knot on the right strand to keep a gap of approximately 70cm (27¹/₂in) between the centre motif of the necklace and the plum blossom knot at the end of the strand.

Tie a four-unit ball ring knot with the end on the left around the strand at the top of the plum blossom knot. Tighten the ring knot against the plum blossom knot and trim the excess close to the ring knot. Repeat for the other end of the necklace.

New dawn

Materials required
To make one 70cm (27¹/₂in) necklace:
• 2m (78¹/₂in) fine cord in sea green
• 1 traditional, embroidered Korean medallion

Featured knots
Lotus, see page 18.
Ring (four-unit ball),
see page 22.
Chrysanthemum,
see page 62.

Centre motif

Tie a lotus knot in the centre of your cord, having located the centre as described in the instructions for the lotus knot (see step 1, page 18). Move to the tightening and adjusting stage and shorten the loop at the top, ensuring that the two strands stay the same length. Using your hook (see page 10), thread the two strands into the hole at the bottom of the pendant and bring them out at the top. Arrange your work so the pendant is at the top with the strands facing down towards you.

Make up a lotus knot, using the pendant as a starting knot. Tighten the lotus knot against the pendant. Tie a chrysanthemum knot, using the last lotus knot you tied as a starting knot. Tighten the chrysanthemum knot against this lotus knot, then tie another lotus knot, using the chrysanthemum knot as your starting knot. Tighten it against the top of the chrysanthemum.

Sliding clasp: first half

Lay the two ends out vertically in front of you, with your work right side up. Place the right strand over your left index finger, leaving the end out to the left. Take the left strand approximately 35cm (13³/₄in) from the lotus knot at the top of the centre motif and tie a four-unit ball ring knot around the right strand and your left index finger.

Sliding clasp: second half

Turn your work over on to the reverse. Pull the loose end through the ring knot and tie a second ring knot to the right of the first, 35cm (13³/₄in) from the lotus knot, around the other strand. Avoid twisting your cord.

Finishing off

If needed, move the two ring knots along the strands so they lie equidistant, 35cm (13³/₄in) from the centre motif. Ensure that the knots slide easily along the strands and trim the excess cord from each knot.

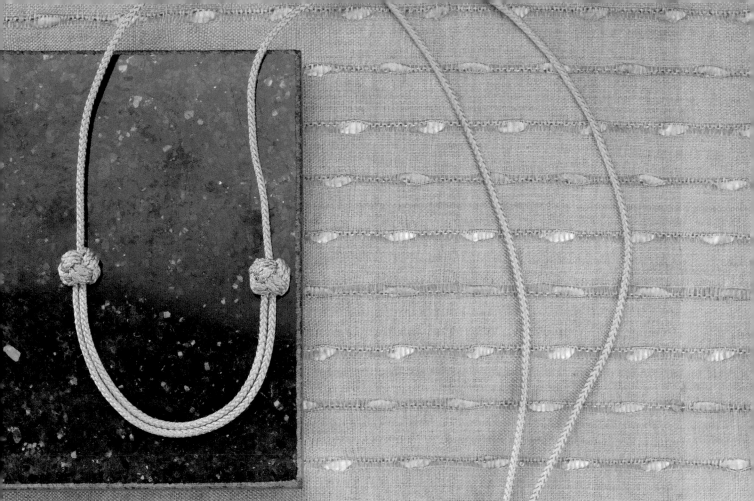

Jade camaïeu

Materials required

To make one 60cm (23¹/₂in) necklace:
• 2 x 2m (78¹/₂in) Japanese cord in
varying shades of beige and brown
• 1 jade pendant

Featured knots
Double connection,
see page 14.
Lotus, see page 18.
Ring (four-unit ball),
see page 22.
Chick, see page 72.

Pendant assembly

Thread the pendant into the centre of one of the two lengths of cord and tie a double connection knot.

Centre motif

Tie a lotus knot at the centre of the second cord and start to tighten and adjust each of the strands. Just before you tighten the knot completely, bring the two loose ends up to the top, then, using your hook (see page 10), insert the two ends from the double connection knot into the lotus. Tighten the lotus knot and bring it close to the double connection knot: you should now have four strands at the top of your work.

Tie a chick knot with two strands on either side rather than one. Tighten the knot against the lotus knot. At the top of the chick knot, locate the two outer strands and the two central strands. Turn your work over so the loose ends are at the bottom and tie a lotus knot with the two outer strands, using the chick knot as your starting knot. Start to tighten and adjust each of the strands. Just before you tighten the knot completely, use your hook to thread the two central strands from the chick knot into the lotus knot. Tighten the knot and push it up against the top of the chick knot. Tie a double connection knot, with two strands on each side, on top of the lotus knot.

Sliding clasp: first half

Lay your work out right side up and with all the loose ends vertically in front of you. Place the right strands over your left index finger, leaving the ends out to the left. Take the left strands 30cm (12in) from the last double connection knot. Tie a ring knot with the two left strands around the two right strands and your left index finger: follow the instructions for the four-unit ring knot from step 2 to step 6 (see page 23), working with the two strands at the same time. Ensure the two strands remain parallel. At the end of step 6, skip straight to the tightening and adjusting stage, following the instructions in step 8 (ball version).

Sliding clasp: second half

Turn your work over on to the reverse. Pull the two loose ends through the ring knot for a length of approximately 30cm (12in). Proceed in exactly the same way as for the previous step to make up a ring knot to the right of the first around the two other strands. Ensure that the two knots slide easily along the strands and that they are equidistant, 30cm (12in) from the two double connection knots that sit on top of the centre motif of the necklace. If needed, move them along the strands (see step 8, page 27), working with both strands in the weave at once.

Doubling up the clasp

When the first two ring knots are in place on the necklace, tie another ring knot next to each one, using the same process as in the previous steps. Using your hook (see page 10), thread the loose ends into the last knots you tied, then trim the excess. Hide them in your work using your awl.

Bead necklace 1

Single-colour necklace

Materials required
To make one 40cm (15³/₄in) necklace:
• 5m (197in) fine cord in turquoise

Featured knots
*Double connection,
see page 14.
Ring (four-unit ball),
see page 22.
Butterfly, see page 80.*

Clasp: loop

Locate the centre of your cord and halve it. Leave an approximately 1.5cm (⁵/₈in) loop at the start of your necklace, then tie a double connection knot.

Knots

Tie 25 double connection knots in succession, ensuring they sit tightly against each other. Lay your work out straight in front of you, with the two loose ends towards the top. Tie a butterfly knot, using the last double connection knot as your starting knot. Once you have tightened the butterfly knot, move it against the last double connection knot. Tie 61 more double connection knots.

Clasp: ball

Tie a four-unit ball ring knot, as follows. Place the last double connection knot at the base of your left index finger and follow the instructions for the four-unit ring knot from step 2 to step 6 (see page 23), working with the two strands at the same time. Keep the two strands parallel at all times. At the end of step 6, skip straight to the tightening and adjusting stage, following the instructions in step 8 (ball version). Using your hook (see page 10), thread the loose ends into the knot, then trim them. If needed, hide them in your work using your awl.

Bead necklace 2

Two-colour necklace

Materials required

To make one 48cm (19in) necklace:
- *5m (197in) fine cord in dark pink*
- *60cm (23¹/₂in) fine cord in maroon*

Featured knots

Double connection, see page 14.
Lotus, see page 18.
Ring (four-unit ball), see page 22.
Butterfly, see page 80.

Maroon beads

Make up two four-unit ball ring knots with the maroon cord. Trim the ends close to each knot.

Clasp: loop

Locate the centre of the dark pink cord and halve it. Leave an approximately 1.5cm (⁵/₈in) loop at the start of your necklace, then tie a double connection knot.

Knots

Make up 99 double connection knots in succession, ensuring that the knots sit tightly against each other. Place the loose ends towards the bottom and make up a lotus knot, using the last double connection knot as a starting knot. Tie a second lotus knot. Using your hook (see page 10), thread a ring knot on to the two strands at the same time. Place your work out straight in front of you, with the two loose ends at the top. Tie a butterfly knot, using the ring knot as your starting knot. Once you have tightened the butterfly knot, move it against the ring knot. Thread the second ring knot on to the two strands at the same time at the base of the butterfly. Place the loose ends towards the bottom, then tie a lotus knot, using the ring knot as your starting knot.

Clasp: ball

Tie the ball for the clasp after the lotus knot, using exactly the same process as for the ball for the single-colour necklace clasp (see page 122).

Variant

Just before moving to the tightening and adjusting stage of the butterfly body, insert a translucent sequin approximately 1cm (³/₈in) in diameter or a flat bead between the two sides of your weaving.

Slender butterflies

Bracelet

Materials required

To make one 19cm (7 1/2in) bracelet:
• 2.6m (102 1/2in) fine cord in royal blue

Featured knots

Double connection,
see page 14.
Ring (four-unit ball),
see page 22.
Butterfly, see page 80.

Knots

Tie 16 double connection knots. Place your work out vertically in front of you with the two loose ends towards the top, then tie a butterfly knot, using the last double connection knot as your starting knot. Tie 17 double connection knots after the butterfly.

Clasp: loop

Locate the centre of your cord and halve it. Leave an approximately 1.5cm (5/8in) loop at the start of the bracelet, then tie a double connection knot.

Clasp: ball

Make up the ball for the clasp after the last double connection knot, using exactly the same process as for the ball in the clasp of the single-colour necklace (see page 122).

Brooch

Materials required
• 2.6m (102¹/₂in) soutache braid in maroon
• 60cm (23¹/₂in) fine cord in maroon
• 1 brooch mount
• needle and thread
• glue

Featured knots
*Ring (four-unit ball),
see page 22.
Butterfly, see page 80.*

Butterfly

Tie a length of fine thread in the centre of your soutache braid to mark your starting point and make up a butterfly. Take care not to twist the soutache as you work.

Antennae

After you have tightened your butterfly, bring the loose end located on the bottom right of the butterfly body to the left of the starting point for the knot: using your hook, thread it diagonally into the weave of the butterfly body. A second, smaller loop will form at the bottom right of the butterfly body. Work in the same way with the left strand to form the second antenna. Pull the ends at the top of the butterfly gently to make the two small loops at the bottom of the body identical, then trim the ends to form two 5cm (2in) antennae.

Antennae tips

Take your 60cm (23¹/₂in) fine maroon cord and tie two four-unit ball ring knots. Trim the ends on each side of the knots. Use your hook (see page 10) to thread one ring knot on to each antenna. Apply a little glue to the end of the antennae and place the ring knots on top. Finally, sew your brooch mount to the back of the butterfly.

Suppliers

UK & Europe

Little Beader
(mail order cords, beads etc)
221 London Road, Rayleigh
Essex, SS6 9DN
littlebeader@yahoo.co.uk
www.littlebeader.com

Bead Addict
(mail order cords, beads, embellishments)
Stephanie Lewis-Cooper
8 Charter Close, Sale
Cheshire, M33 5YG
stephanie@beadaddict.com
www.beadaddict.co.uk

Texere Yarns Ltd
(cord in a wide variety of colours)
College Mill, Barkerend Road
Bradford, BD1 4AU
01274 722191
info@texereyarns.co.uk
http://texere.co.uk

eBay
(speciality cord, beads, mounts, findings,
embellishments and more)
www.ebay.co.uk

Mokuba
(Cords and ribbons)
18, rue Montmarte
75001, Paris
+33 (0) 1 40 13 81 41

US

The Satin Cord Store
(range of cords, embellishments, beads
and more)
8132 Renault Drive South
Jacksonville, FL 32244
888 728 8245
or 904 683 4123
www.satincord.com

Rings and Things
(wholesale cords, jewellery
making supplies and more)
P.O. Box 450, Spokane,
WA 99210-0450
800 366 2156
www.rings-things.com

Acknowledgements

Thanks to Moline and Jardin d'Ulysse
for supplying fabrics and accessories for
the styling and photography:

Groupe Moline
(fabrics, haberdashery)
1, place Saint-Pierre
75018 Paris
Tel. +33 (0)1 46 06 14 66
www.tissus-moline.com

Jardin d'Ulysse
(textiles, interiors)
Several outlets in France
Tel. +33 (0)4 72 26 59 59
www.jardindulysse.com

Many thanks also to Lorraine for her inva-
luable help.

About the author

Kim Sang Lan is Korean and has practised
Korean knotwork, which she learnt from
a Korean master, for over thirty years. A
former university lecturer and a graduate in
visual and applied arts, she is a textile artist
of great renown. Now living in France, she
exhibits widely and teaches Korean knot
craft at the Korean Cultural Centre, the
Musée Guimet and the ADAC (Association
for the Development of Cultural Activities)
in Paris.